LITTLE GIANT® ENCYCLOPEDIA

OF

Fortune Telling

THE LITTLE GIANT® ENCYCLOPEDIA

OF

Fortune Telling

THE DIAGRAM GROUP

Sterling Publishing Co., Inc.
New York

Compiled by Jane Johnstone and Maya Pilkington

Library of Congress Cataloging-in-Publication Data

The little giant encyclopedia of fortune telling / the Diagram
group.
     p. cm.
     Includes index.
     ISBN 0-8069-4823-X
     Fortune-telling-Encyclopedias. I. Diagram Group.
BF 1861.L62 1999
133.3'03—dc 21   98–47995
                                       CIP

10 9 8 7 6 5 4 3

Published by Sterling Publishing Company, Inc.
387 Park Avenue South, New York, N.Y. 10016
© 1999 by Diagram Visual Information Limited
Distributed in Canada by Sterling Publishing
C/o Canadian Manda Group, One Atlantic Avenue, Suite 105
Toronto, Ontario, Canada M6K 3E7
Distributed in Australia by Capricorn Link (Australia) Pty Ltd.
P.O. Box 704, Windsor, NSW 2756 Australia
Printed in China

Sterling ISBN 0-8069-4823-X

FOREWORD

Some people take predicting the future seriously; others are skeptical and regard it as a frivolous amusement. Whatever your views, you cannot help but be intrigued by the variety of methods that have been used over the centuries, many of which are still practiced today. *The Little Giant Encyclopedia of Fortune-Telling* brings together the methods of fortune-tellers from past and present, east and west, and explains how and why these forms of divination have been considered worthy of serious study. Well-known methods of predicting, such as astrology, palmistry, and tarot, are described in detail, and techniques and principles are explained in a step-by-step format, enabling you to try out these methods of divination for yourself. Detailed information is also included about many other methods of prediction, including the less well-known and obscure methods such as hydromancy (prediction using water), geomancy (prediction using the earth), and scrying (prediction using a reflective surface).

Whether you want to find out more about the bumps on your head (phrenology) or how to read tea leaves (tasseography); if you are intrigued by old wives' tales or fascinated by numbers; or if you simply want to find out more about the meaning of your dreams (oneiromancy), you will find *The Little Giant Encyclopedia of Fortune-Telling* a fascinating read.

CONTENTS

AEROMANCY AND HYDROMANCY

Definition Aeromancy (divination by atmospheric conditions) and hydromancy (divination by water) are two methods of fortune-telling that are closely related. Aeromancy includes almost anything occurring in the sky, such as winds, storms, clouds, and rainbows, each type of aeromancy having a different name.

Forms of aeromancy

Name	Divination using:
Austromancy (**a**)	the study of winds.
Ceraunoscopy (**b**)	thunder and lightning.
Chaomancy (**c**)	aerial visions.
Meteormancy (**d**)	meteors and shooting stars.

a

b

c

d

History Aeromancy and hydromancy are ancient forms of divination. Hindus interpreted the shapes made in clouds, while thunder and lightning particularly intrigued the Etruscans and Babylonians, who worshipped the gods of weather. Later, some societies observed the effects of wind on everyday objects—for example, bells were sometimes hung in a tree and the sounds of their ringing interpreted. Hydromancy played

Gods of aeromancy and hydromancy

God	Area of influence
Tin	Etruscan god of thunder and lightning. Sometimes known as Tinia, this god was later associated with the Roman god Jupiter. Tin had three thunderbolts—the first two were hurled as a warning, the third as a punishment.
Ea	All-seeing and all-knowing, Ea was a Babylonian god of fresh water and magic incantations.
Adad	Another Babylonian god of thunder and lightning, also the god of prophecy.
Hapi	An Egyptian god of the deified Nile, sometimes worshipped in the form of the bull-god Apis.

an important role in divination for some societies and ripples made in water were thought to be of particular importance. Pebbles or precious stones were dropped into a sacred pool and the size, speed, and number of ripples observed. The shape of stones was also varied: a seer would first drop a round stone, then a triangular one, then a cube.

Drinking the water from sacred springs was another form of hydromancy. Such activity was thought to cause madness but also to induce prophetic visions. Gazing into bowls or pools of still water was also used, and is a form of scrying (described later in this book).

Practicing aeromancy

Method 1
1 Take two pieces of paper the same size, shape, and weight, one colored black and the other left white.
2 Concentrate on a question for which you require a "yes" or a "no" answer.
3 Drop both pieces of paper from an upstairs window and see which touches the ground first.
If the white paper touches the ground first, the answer to your question will be yes.

Method 2
1 Take several small pieces of paper, all of the same size, shape, and weight.
2 Consider all the possible answers to your question and write each one on one of the pieces of paper.
3 Place the pieces of paper face down on a table and switch on an electric fan.
The first piece of paper to be blown off the table and to fall face up on the floor reveals your answer.

Modern methods Most of the methods of aeromancy and hydromancy have become obscure and are little practiced today. However, some elements of these forms of fortune-telling can be found in prevailing supersitions and folklore. For example, there is a European superstition that thunder in the east foretells bloodshed, and that the death of a king is prophesied by a high wind at Christmas or Epiphany.

Equipment You can practice aeromancy and hydromancy using some very simple equipment. The methods described here require some small pieces of colored paper, a bowl of water and an electric fan.

Practicing hydromancy

Method 1

1 Concentrate on a questinon for which you need a
   "yes" or "no" answer.
2 Drop a pebble into a bowl of water and count the
   ripples.

An even number of ripples means the answer to your
question is "no"; an odd number and the answer is
"yes."

Method 2

To know the name of your future partner:

1 Think of as many names as you can for possible partners.
2 Write one name on each of many separate sheets of paper of the same size, shape, and weight.
3 Roll each piece of paper into a ball.
4 Hold them all together in the air as far above your head as possible, then let them fall together into a bowl of water.

The first piece of paper to float to the top will carry the name of your future partner.

AUGURY

Definition A method of divination based mainly on the behavior and appearance of animals. Each means of prediction has a different name (see table on page 16).

History In Roman times, the wishes of the gods and almost any plan of action were ascertained by the college of augurs, who read omens in almost everything. The most common method of augury was ornithomancy, predicting from the sound, appearance, and flight of birds. Wearing a ritual toga, the augur stood on a hilltop, facing south, and pointed to the area of sky he was going to use for his predictions, using a special wooden staff. Interpreting signs was complex. Signs occurring on the augur's right were considered unfavorable; the reverse was true for those occurring on his left. The speed of flight, the number of birds, the nature of their droppings, and whether they shed any feathers were all factors to be taken into account. Furthermore, different birds were consulted in a different way. The voices of crows, hens, owls, and ravens were thought to reveal the wishes of the gods, whilst with eagles and vultures, flight patterns were considered significant.

Modern methods Augury survives today in the form of omens and superstitions, especially those relating to animals (see pages 16–17).

Haruspicy

This is sometimes considered to be part of augury and involves predicting the future from the appearance of the entrails of animals, usually those dedicated and sacrificed to the gods. Some haruspices claimed to be able to tell the state of the intestines from the outward appearance of an animal alone, others consulted not only the intestines but also the spleen, kidneys, lungs, gall bladder, and liver. Haruspicy was practiced by the Assyrians, the Babylonians, and the Etruscans, by tribes in Africa and Borneo, and by the Aztecs. The liver was considered to be of particular importance, and hepatoscopy (divination by the liver) was a highly respected art. Models of the liver date back as far as 2000 B.C. divided into forty or so zones, each governed by a separate god. Textures, marks, and veins would all have had their own specific meanings, depending on their location.

a The giant Humbaba, with his head formed of intestines, was an important figure in Assyrian divination.
b Clay tablet used by the Babylonians to show the meanings of the intestines of sheep.
c Babylonian clay model of the liver.

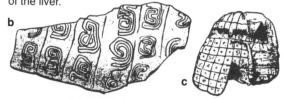

Means of prediction used by augurs

Name	Prediction using:
Ophiomancy (**a**)	the color and movement of snakes.
Myomancy (**b**)	the color and movement of mice.
Entomomancy (**c**)	the appearance and behavior of insects.
Arachnomancy (**d**)	the appearance and behavior of spiders.
Cephalomancy	the skull or head of a donkey or goat.
Ichthyomancy (**e**)	the shape and entrails of fish.
Alectryomancy (**f**)	the eating patterns of sacred chickens.
Phyllorhodomancy	rose petals.
Oenomancy	the patterns made by wine poured out as an offering to the gods.
Scapulomancy	the patterns or cracks and fissures on the burned shoulder blade of an animal.
Tephromancy	the patterns in the ashes of burnt offerings made to the gods.
Zoomancy	the appearance and behavior of animals.

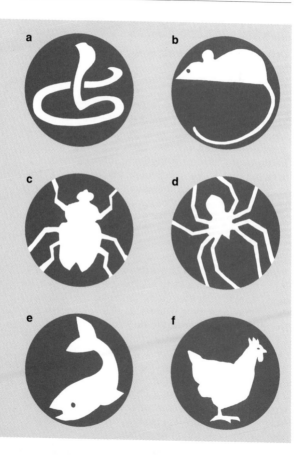

CARTOMANCY

Definition Using modern playing cards to predict the future.

History Modern playing cards were evolved from tarot cards, and the current deck—of French origin—probably originated in the late fifteenth century.

Modern methods Card interpretations vary between sources. The interpretations shown here are those most generally accepted today.

Equipment Cards were originally either painted by hand or printed with woodblocks, and designed to be viewed from one direction only (as tarot cards still are). In 1832 playing cards were mass produced and are widely available all over the world. To practice cartomancy yourself, you will need a standard deck of 52 playing cards.

Preparing to read the cards

It is considered unlucky to read the cards when you are alone, to read your own cards, or to read the cards of the same subject more than once in the same week.

Deciding whether or not to do a full reading

1 Choose the client card for your subject and place it in the middle of the table.

2 The subject then shuffles the cards and cuts them into three with the left hand.

3 Read the bottom card of each of the stacks, first separately, and then in combination.

4 On the basis of this first reading, decide whether the time is propitious for a full reading.

The client card

This is a king or queen selected by the reader to represent the person who is the subject of the reading. You should try to choose a card that matches your subject's age, sex, and hair color, as far as this is possible.

Subject	Card to use
Fair, gray, or auburn-haired older man	King of diamonds
Fair, gray, or auburn-haired older woman	Queen of diamonds
Fair or auburn-haired younger man	King of hearts
Fair or auburn-haired younger woman	Queen of hearts
Dark-haired older man	King of spades
Dark-haired older woman	Queen of spades
Dark-haired younger man	King of clubs
Dark-haired younger woman	Queen of clubs

Making a full reading
Deciding whether or not to do a full reading

1 Keep the client card in the middle of the table.

2 Ask your subject to shuffle the cards again and to cut them into three, using the left hand.

3 With both you and the client concentrating on the cards, arrange them around the client card in either the Seven Triplets or Lucky 13 layouts.

4 Begin your reading, using the tables here to help you.

Lucky 13 layout
Used to give a general picture of the future, or to answer a question about a specific area of the client's life. The client card is always the joker.

- Deal the first 12 cards of the pack, face down, in the order shown by the numbers on the diagram below.
- Turn the cards face up and interpret them, using the tables provided.

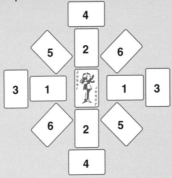

Seven Triplets layout (also known as The Seven)
- Deal out the first 21 cards, face down, in the order shown by the numbers in the diagram.
- Beginning on the left, turn up each pack of three cards and interpret them, using the tables provided.

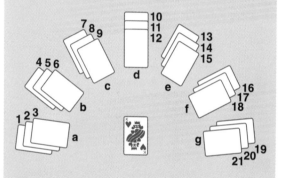

- Take into account the area of influence represented by each of the seven packs:

a Personality and state of mind.
b Family and home.
c Present desires.
d Hopes and expectations.
e The unexpected.
f The immediate future.
g The more distant future.

CARD INTERPRETATION
The influence of suits

You may find that when laying out the cards, one suit is more strongly represented than the others. It is important that you take this into account in your reading as each suit is said to have its own particular area of influence. The impression conveyed by the prominent suit should be used to modify your interpretation of the other cards.

Suit	Influence
Hearts ♥	Domestic life—love, affection, friendship, marriage, the family. Hearts also stand for ambitions successfully realized and are considered lucky.
Clubs ♣	Success—with money, business, and loyalty; failure, betrayal, and financial worries.
Diamonds ♦	Life outside the home. They also suggest that ambitions can only be realized and money made through hard work.
Spades ♠	Misfortunes—loss, suffering, enemies, treachery, failure. They warn of dangers ahead.

HEARTS CARD INTERPRETATION

Card	Predicts
Ace	The home, love, friendship, and happiness
King	A good-natured, impetuous, fair-haired man
Queen	A trustworthy, affectionate, fair-haired woman
Jack	A close friend
Ten	Good fortune and happiness
Nine	"The wish card" that makes dreams come true
Eight	Invitations and festivities
Seven	False hopes and broken promises, an unreliable person
Six	An overgenerous disposition, unexpected good fortune
Five	Jealousy, indecisiveness
Four	Changes, delays, and postponements (especially of marriages)
Three	Warns of a need for caution
Two	Success and prosperity

CLUBS CARD INTERPRETATION

Card	Predicts
Ace	Wealth, health, love, and happiness
King	An honest, generous, dark-haired man
Queen	An attractive, self-confident, dark-haired woman
Jack	A reliable friend
Ten	Unexpected money, good luck
Nine	Friends being stubborn
Eight	Opposition, disappointment, the taking of reckless chances
Seven	Prosperity—providing a member of the opposite sex does not interfere
Six	Business success
Five	A new friend or a successful marriage
Four	Fortunes changing for the worse
Three	Marriage bringing money. May indicate several marriages
Two	Opposition and disappointments

DIAMONDS CARD INTERPRETATION

Card	Predicts
Ace	Money, a letter, or a ring
King	A stubborn, quick-tempered, fair-haired man
Queen	A flirtatious, sophisticated, fair-haired woman
Jack	A relative, not altogether reliable
Ten	Marriage or money, a journey, changes
Nine	Restlessness. A surprise connected with money
Eight	A marriage late in life. A journey leading to a new relationship
Seven	Heavy losses
Six	A warning against a second marriage
Five	Prosperity, good news, a happy family
Four	An inheritance, changes, troubles
Three	Legal or domestic disputes
Two	A serious love affair

SPADES CARD INTERPRETATION

Card	Predicts
Ace	Emotional conflict, an unfortunate love affair. Sometimes regarded as the "death card"
King	An ambitious dark-haired man
Queen	An unscrupulous dark-haired woman
Jack	A well-meaning but lazy acquaintance
Ten	Misfortune and worry
Nine	Bad luck in all things
Eight	Trouble and disappointment ahead
Seven	Sorrow, loss of friendship
Six	Some improvement in circumstances
Five	Reverses and anxieties, but eventual success
Four	Jealousy, illness, business worries
Three	Faithlessness and partings
Two	Separation, scandal, deceit

SPECIAL COMBINATIONS INTERPRETATION

Some combinations of cards have special meanings when the deck of 52 cards is used. These meanings apply only when the cards are immediately next to one another in the layout.

Card	Predicts
Ace of hearts next to any other heart	Friendship
Ace of hearts with another heart on each side	Love affair
Ace of hearts with a diamond on each side	Money
Ace of hearts with a spade on each side	Quarrels
Ace of diamonds/eight of clubs	Business proposal
Ace of spades/king of clubs	A politician
Ace of spades/ten of spades	A serious undertaking
Ace of spades/four of hearts	A new baby

SPECIAL COMBINATIONS INTERPRETATION

Card	Predicts
Ten of hearts	Cancels adjacent cards of ill fortune; reinforces adjacent cards of good fortune
Ten of diamonds/two of hearts	Marriage bringing money
Ten of spades	Cancels adjacent cards of good fortune; reinforces adjacent cards of ill fortune
Ten of spades next to any club	Business troubles
Ten of spades with a club on each side	Theft, forgery, grave business losses
Nine of hearts next to any card of ill fortune	Quarrels, temporary obstacles
Nine of hearts/five of spades	Loss of status
Nine of clubs/eight of hearts	Gaiety
Nine of diamonds next to any court card	Lack of success, an inability to concentrate

(continued)

Card	Predicts
Nine of diamonds/eight of spades	A bitter quarrel
Nine of spades/seven of diamonds	Loss of money
Eight of hearts/eight of diamonds	A trousseau
Eight of hearts/five of hearts	A present of jewelry
Eight of diamonds/five of hearts	A present of money
Eight of spades on the immediate right of the client card	Abandon your current plans
Four of hearts next to any court card	Many love affairs
Four of clubs next to any court card	A loss, injustice
Two of clubs/two of diamonds	An unexpected message

CLAIRVOYANCE

Definition Clairvoyance means "clear seeing." It is divination by seeing the future ahead of time. Clairvoyance is classed by some as a form of extrasensory perception, of which there are certain other, related types (see chart below).

History Clairvoyant talents have been used by oracles, seers, witch doctors, soothsayers, and shamans for centuries. Cassandra, said to have been given the gift of sight by Apollo, ordained that her prophecies should never be believed. One of the greatest seers of all time was Michel de Notredame (1503–1566), better known

Types of extrasensory perception

Type	meaning
Clairaudience	"Clear hearing" and is divination by hearing the future ahead of time.
Psychometry	Clairvoyant divination about a specific person through holding an object belonging to that person.
Metagnomy	Divination by sights of future events seen when in a hypnotic trance.
Precognition	Inner paranormal knowledge of the future.

as Nostradamus (see page 298). One of the best known American clairvoyants is Jeane Dixon, who predicted the assassination of President Kennedy.

Modern methods Some argue that all forms of predicting the future are ultimately dependent on clairvoyance. Forms of predicting which might help you develop any latent talent include tasseography (**a**), crystallomancy (**b**), reading the tarot (**c**), radiesthesia (**d**), captoptromance (**e**), and palmistry (**f**).

Equipment The equipment required depends on what form of clairvoyance you practice—tasseography requires used tea leaves, for example, cartomancy requires playing cards, etc.

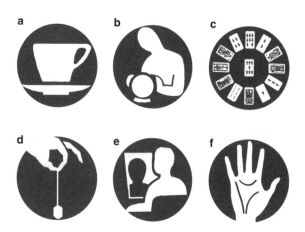

Developing clairvoyance

It is assumed by many that you either have the gift of
clairvoyance or you do not. Some authorities, however,
now believe clairvoyant ability is a widespread human
potential—such as intuition—and that everyone has it
to some extent, even if it is latent, lying undiscovered.
This belief stems from cases involving ordinary people
with no previous history of psychic ability, who, at
moments of unusual stress, have had precognitive
experiences.

Some clairvoyants assert that latent abilities can be
activated and various methods have been suggested for
how this might be achieved.

Method	Uses in developing clairvoyance
Meditation	Deep forms of meditation may help to relax the mind, shed the restrictions of rationalist and materialist thinking, and put you in touch with the deeper levels of your psyche.
Use of tools	A tool may help to concentrate non-rational areas of the mind.
Hypnosis	To help you attune to a semi-trance state that clears away barriers, helping to get in touch with the intuitive, paranormal mental areas.

Future predictions
Some events predicted to occur before the end of this century by present-day clairvoyants.

1 Discovery of a vaccine against cancer.
2 A manned landing on Mars.
3 A single currency in use throughout the world.
4 A total ban on all cigarettes.
5 Discovery of Atlantis.
6 The beginning of a new ice age.
7 Discovery of life on planets outside the solar system.
8 Russia becoming a Christian country.

DICE

Definition Small cubes with numbered sides ("faces") which are often used to provide random numbers in games of chance.

History Dice have existed since at least 2000 B.C. and seem to have been universally popular all over the world. The use of dice for divination probably evolved from sortilege, which is divination by the casting of lots. Astragalomancy is a form of sortilege that used astragals, the vertebrae or the ankle bones of sheep. As they had four easily-distinguishable faces, they were convenient for throwing—each face could be given a set value. In ancient Greece and Rome, astragals persisted in use alongside more recognizable forms of dice until the tenth century.

Modern methods A modern method of using dice to predict the future is to throw two or three dice into a circle and interpret the results.

Equipment Dice have been made in a variety of forms and shapes, sometimes with up to 20 faces. Many were made of wood, bone, or ivory, although more precious materials have also been used and were thought to enhance the power of the dice. Modern dice are usually cubes made of plastic with markings on each of the faces. The standard western marking uses spots to represent numbers, with a 1-spot opposite the 6-spot face, the 2 is opposite 5, and 3 opposite 4. However, other numberings still occur in other parts of the world.

Early dice

a Astragal
b Ancient Egyptian die
c Etruscan die
d Roman long die, marked *malest* (ill luck) on one side
e Roman die with 14 faces
f Die in the form of a six-sided figurine
g Asian long-dice

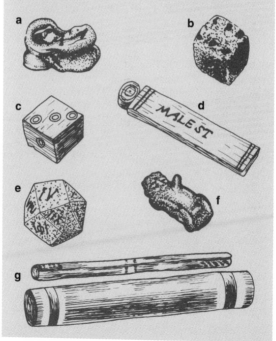

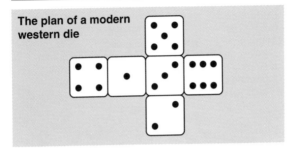

The plan of a modern western die

ASTRAGALOMANCY

This is a form of divination using two dice that allows you to answer a specific question by throwing dice into a circle. Originally a pair of astragals (probably the left and right ankle-bones of sheep) would have been used.

1 Draw a circle.
2 Concentrate on your question.
3 Throw the dice into the circle.
4 Add the numbers on the two dice and consult the list of answers below. If a die falls outside a circle it is not counted.

Total	Meaning	Total	Meaning
One	Yes	Seven	Have faith
Two	No	Eight	Be patient
Three	Take care	Nine	Certainly
Four	Be wise	Ten	Doubtful
Five	Good luck	Eleven	Nonsense
Six	Of course	Twelve	A chance

DIVINATION USING THREE DICE

You will need three dice, a large piece of paper and a pencil on which to draw a large circle. Alternatively, you can scratch a circle into the earth using a sharp stick. You may also prefer to throw dice from a small cup rather than your hand.

1 Draw your circle. This should be about 12 inches (30 cm) in diameter.

2 Throw the dice.

3 Add together the numbers on the three dice and look up the meaning of the total on pages 40–41. Count only those dice that fall within the circle.

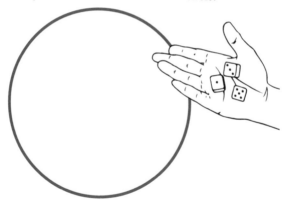

If a number recurs during reading, it indicates that significant news is on the way.

If one die lands on top of another and stays there, you may receive a gift—but you must take care, both in business and love.

If any dice fall outside the circle

If all three fall outside the circle, try again. If the dice fall outside the circle a second time, do not throw them again—wait for a more propitious time.

Position of dice	Prediction
If one die falls outside the circle	Add together the two dice but remember your plans may go wrong
If two dice land outside the circle	Trouble or a quarrel may be coming
If a die falls on the floor	There may be troubled times ahead
Two dice on the floor	Suggest serious trouble
If one or more dice land outside the circle and the remaining dice total less than three	There is no reading – only the numbers from three to 18 are read

Examples of possible throws

Interpreting the totals

Total	Prediction
3	A surprise or some unexpected news may be on the way, but it will be favorable.
4	Disappointment or unpleasantness could be in store, and possibly bad luck, too.
5	Your wish will come true, but perhaps in an unexpected way. A stranger may bring happiness.
6	There will be loss and misfortune, probably in money and business matters.
7	You will suffer setbacks and maybe unhappiness through scandal or gossip—be careful.
8	Outside influences are strong, and you might be the victim of unfair blame or injustice.
9	Lucky for love and marriage; you can expect reconciliation and forgiveness after a quarrel.
10	A strong prediction of birth, also domestic happiness and a promotion or business success.

Total	Prediction
11	A parting, perhaps from someone close to you; there may be an illness.
12	Good news will arrive, probably by letter, and you should take advice before replying.
13	This dark number predicts grief and sorrow, which may last a very long time.
14	A friend will help you, or you may meet a new admirer or stranger who will become a close friend.
15	You need to take great care, perhaps against some temptation into dishonesty.
16	This number tells of travel, and the omens for the journey are very good.
17	A change of plan may come about through a person from overseas or who is associated with water.
18	This number is the best omen of all, bringing success, prosperity, and happiness.

Specific predictions

By dividing your throwing circle into 12 equal sections
the overall message gained from the total of the
numbers on the dice can now be applied to particular
areas of your life. In addition, a special prediction can
be made for each section by reading the number on the
individual die within it. If two or three dice fall into the
same section, this makes the message much more
forceful. Using the chart opposite, interpret the
numbers on the individual dice as shown below, and
integrate these meanings with your earlier readings to
give a coherent prediction.

Interpreting individual die numbers		
·	**1**	Generally favorable, but bear the overall prediction in mind
· ·	**2**	Your success depends on your friends
· · ·	**3**	An excellent omen for success
· · · ·	**4**	Disappointment and trouble
· · · · ·	**5**	Good indications
· · · · · ·	**6**	Uncertainty

Interpreting sections of the circle

A Next year
B Money matters
C Travel
D Domestic matters
E The present
F Health
G Love and marriage
H Legal matters
I Your present state of mind
J Work and career
K Friends
L Enemies

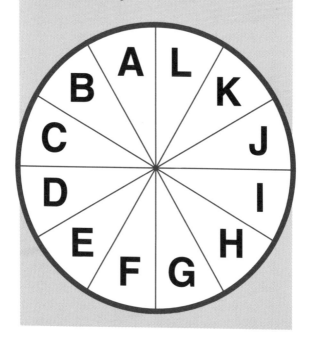

DOMINOES

Definition Dominoes are small, oblong-shaped tiles of wood, ivory or plastic on which appear combinations of dots from which predictions can be made about the future.

History Although dominoes are used almost exclusively in the west for game playing, they would probably have been for used for divination in twelfth-century China, where they were first recorded, perhaps evolving as a form of dice. In the east, mystic names were given to the tiles such as "The Little Snakes," and "Leaping Gazelle." These names no longer exist for western dominoes. European dominoes probably came from China and first appeared in Italy and France in the eighteenth century. Their name may have derived from a long black cloak and face mask called a domino.

Modern methods In India and Korea dominoes are still used for prediction, and some Indian and Chinese games involve both gambling and fortune telling. You can practice reading the dominoes using a standard western-style set.

A three-five spot domino

Equipment A set of western style dominoes consists of 28 tiles. Each tile is divided in half, and each half has spots indicating numbers from zero to six. Sets running up to nine–nine or even 12–12 do exist but are rare. Chinese dominoes have 32 pieces and are marked with red and black spots. They consist of 11 identical pairs, 10 single dominoes, and no blanks.

How to read the dominoes

1 Lay the tiles face down.

2 Shuffle them.

3 Pick only three dominoes at a time using either of the two methods described on the next page.

4 Never consult the dominoes more than once a week.

Method 1
1 Pick your first domino and put it aside.
2 Shuffle the set.
3 Pick your second domino and put it aside also.
4 Shuffle the set.
5 Pick your third domino.
6 Consult the tables here to obtain your fortune from
   the three dominoes you have picked.

Method 2
1 Pick your first domino and consult the tables for its
   meaning.
2 Return your first domino to the set.
3 Shuffle the set.
4 Pick your second domino and consult the tables
   for its meaning.
5 Return the second domino to the set.
6 Shuffle the set.
7 Pick your third domino and consult the tables for
   its meaning.
Using this method means that the same domino may
be picked more than once. If that happens, the
prophecy will be fulfilled quickly.

Domino meanings

Domino	Meaning
	The best domino in the set: strong omens for success and happiness in every area of life.
	A close friend or benefactor; patience and perseverance; a kind action will bring you great reward.
	Quarrel, perhaps a lawsuit with an unsuccessful outcome.
	You will travel, or a journey will affect your life. A holiday will be happy; a journey may bring a gift.

Domino meanings (continued)

Domino	Meaning
	Very good luck is coming your way; your circumstances may be improved. This tile is only lucky for the honest.
	An end to your problems; a good friend could be involved in this. A wedding.
	Be careful of false friends or a deceitful person. You could suffer some unhappiness because of gossip.
	Change that brings success. You might move to a new place where you will be happy, or make money from a new idea.

Domino	Meaning
	Profits and good fortune in material terms, possibly unexpected. Don't take any chances—it's not a good time for investments.
	A calm and well-adjusted atmosphere. You will get some good news or advice from a visitor or your boss.
	A true friend will have an influence on your life. Also an omen for birth.
	A love affair, or an interesting meeting with a new friend. Things may not end happily for those in love.

Domino meanings (continued)

Domino	Meaning
	Some sadness—you may have to give comfort to a friend in trouble. You need caution, so think carefully about what you say.
	Happiness, fun, relaxation, celebration. There may be a party in a big building.
	You might have expected some problems or disappointments, but instead will find happiness and success.
	A change of some sort, but not a happy one—setbacks, losses, or maybe even a robbery. Someone you know is deceitful—be careful.

Domino	Meaning
	Some financial problems ahead—be sure that you pay any outstanding debts.
	Some news will not be favorable—you may be disappointed in a love affair; something you want could be postponed. Try to reconcile a quarrel.
	Obstacles in your emotional life—jealousy or distress. Money is well favored.
	Pleasant change may be coming, but you need to be cautious just now, especially in financial matters.

Domino meanings (continued)

Domino	Meaning
	The answer to the question in your mind is "no." Some surprising news may be useful, but beware of unhappiness caused by outsiders.
	Unexpected problems both at home and at work.
	You will get what you want. Business success and personal happiness are predicted, but enemies might try to spoil it for you.
	Financial problems and maybe a loss of money or property. However, this domino is good for social life and friends.

Domino	Meaning
	A good omen for travel and meeting new friends, but something is worrying you and someone could cause difficulties for you.
	Harmony and affection are predicted, and a stranger could be involved. You have an important decision to make—don't put it off.
	A stranger or outsider will bring some interesting news that could mean financial gain, but don't be too trusting.
	This domino has a negative effect on all your activities.

DOWSING

Definition Method of divination used to locate things under the earth, including water, mineral deposits, bodies, archeological sites, cables, pipes and tunnels, lost property and hidden treasure. Use of a pendulum (radiesthesia) is a form of indoor dowsing.

History A cave painting in the northern Sahara dating back to at least 6000 B.C. shows a man holding a forked stick in much the same way as a modern diviner. Dowsers also occur in early Chinese, Egyptian, and Peruvian carvings. In the period between the fifteenth and seventeenth centuries, dowsers were often attached to the staff of prospecting and mining expeditions and searched mainly for metal. During the eighteenth and nineteenth centuries they looked mainly for water.

Modern methods Today, public corporations sometimes use dowsers to pinpoint unmapped cables and pipelines.

Equipment For dowsing out of doors you will need either a traditional forked twig or a modern divining rod. Some dowsers like to carry a sample with them. This should be large enough to come in contact with both your skin and the rod, but small enough to carry comfortably. Liquids may be carried in a small bottle but a sample is not usually needed when searching for water, as its influence is so powerful. For dowsing indoors you will need some form of pendulum.

Choosing a dowsing twig

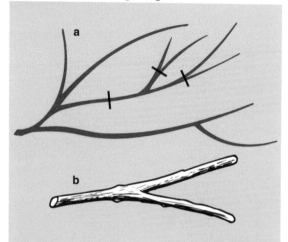

- The best type of wood to use is hazel, but beech, apple, birch, willow and privet can also be used. Whichever wood you choose, make sure it isn't brittle and that it doesn't break easily. Your twig should be pliable, young wood (but not green).

- Find an undamaged, Y-shaped twig, with a strong joint at the Y (**a**). It should be even, and about 3/8 in (1cm) in diameter.
- Cut your twig from the branch.
- Trim the twig (**b**), but leave the bark on.

Making metal divining rods

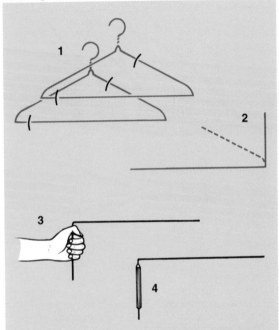

You will need two wire coat hangers.

1 Cut through the coat hangers as shown.
2 Bend each piece of wire into a right angle.

3 Hold each rod as it is, or
4 Make a sleeve by removing the refill and stopper from an old ballpoint pen.

DOWSING OUTDOORS

1 Hold your dowsing twig firmly, with your palms pointing upward and your thumbs pointing outward (**a**), then move your fists apart until the twig is tensed but balanced. If you are using metal divining rods, hold them loosely in clenched fists, with your thumbs resting over your forefingers (**b**). Whichever type of rod you are using, your arms should be in the same horizontal plane as the rod, with elbows tucked well in.

2 Concentrate your mind on the substance you are searching for.

3 Cover the area you are searching methodically, walking slowly and steadily.

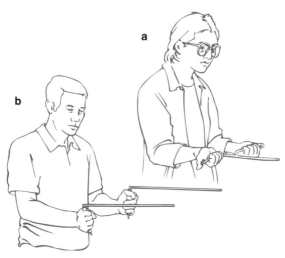

4 Use markers to indicate the places where your rods or
twig reacted. The twig may turn up, down (**c**), or may
revolve completely. The rods will react by crossing, or
swinging apart (**d**).

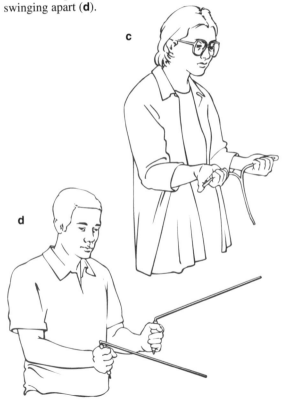

USING A PENDULUM (RADIESTHESIA)

Some dowsers prefer to work indoors, using a pendulum instead of a divining twig or rods. This is known as radiesthesia and can take several different forms, including coscinomancy (divination by sieve), cleidomancy (divination with a suspended key) and dactylomancy (divination with a suspended ring).

Improvising a pendulum

Pendulums can be made in any material, and be any size or shape. Many household objects have been used, some of which are shown here.

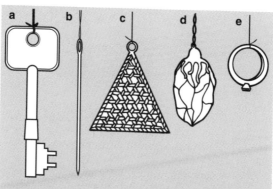

a A key tied to a piece of thin string.

b A large needle on a thread.

c A pendant or medallion.

d A carved crystal on a gold chain.

e A wedding ring suspended on a human hair.

Commercial pendulums

Some dowsers prefer their pendulums to be made of
natural materials, especially wood. Average-sized
commercial pendulums are about 1–2 in (2–5 cm) in
diameter and 1–2 in (2–5 cm) long. Some are designed
to hold whatever substance is being searched for.
Examples of commercially available pendulums are
shown here.

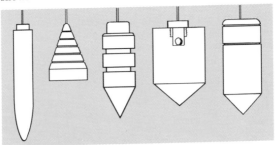

Using a pendulum

Some radiesthesists practice forms of medical
divination. The commonest use of radiesthesia on the
human body is in attempting to detect the sex of an
unborn child.

1 Hold the pendulum in your dominant hand, the hair
between thumb and forefinger, allowing the thumb and
forefinger to form a circle while the other fingers face
down.

2 For some, the pendulum will swing backward and
forward (**a**) to indicate a man or boy; in a circle (**b**) to
indicate a girl or a woman. For other people, the reverse
is true.

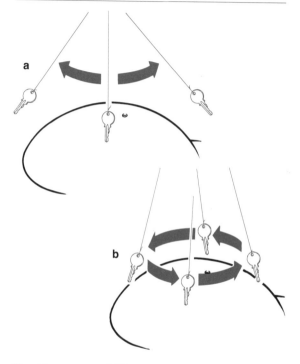

Testing your skills as a radiesthesist

Because pendulums react differently according to the user, it is worth practicing your skill by attempting to locate different substances, and by asking simple questions in order to determine the action of your pendulum for "yes" and "no" responses.

FORTUNES FROM FOOD

Definition Different terms were applied to divination using different foods.

History Alphitomancy was a form of food divination used by seers to detect lies or dishonesty. Special cakes made of wheat or barley flour were supposed to choke liars or wrongdoers but were easily swallowed by those with a clear conscience. Tyromancy was divination from cheese and crithomancy involved reading the markings on freshly baked bread or cakes. Holidays where food and feasting played an important part— such as May Day, Candlemas and Twelfth Night—date from pagan times and have since been absorbed into the Christian tradition. Divination from food was thought to work best on one or more of these feast days. Halloween—the pagan's New Year's Eve—was also the day dedicated to Pomona, the Roman goddess of the orchards, and so apples came to play a significant role in Halloween divination rites.

Modern methods Many forms of divination by food are no longer practiced, although some of the more popular methods are described here.

Equipment All you require are the foods you are going to use for divination.

Divination from peas and beans

On Care Sunday (the fifth Sunday in Lent, now called Passion Sunday) hide a small bean in a large dish of peas to be served with the main meal.

- The person who finds the bean on his or her plate will be the first to marry.

Divination from nuts

To know if your lover is true
Place two nuts in the embers of a fire or on the bars of the grate. These represent yourself and your lover.
- If the nuts jump away from one another, flare up fiercely, or explode, the relationship will be ended by the person whose nut jumps or flares up first.
- If the nuts burn quietly together your relationship will be a long and happy one.

To discover the occupation of your future partner
Chop together a single hazelnut and a single walnut. Grate a piece of nutmeg. Mix them all together with damp bread or a little dough. Form the mixture into nine small pills. Swallow all of the pills before going to bed.
- Your dreams will reveal to you the occupation of your future partner.

Divination from eggs

Egg rolling

Rolling eggs on Easter Day is said to foretell luck and marriage and requires a group of people to participate. You will need a colored hard-boiled egg for each person, marked with their initials or some other identifying mark. Take the eggs to the top of a sloping grassy field and release them at the same time to roll down the hill.

- The first egg to reach the bottom indicates who will marry first.
- Those whose eggs reach the bottom unscathed will have good luck for the next year.
- Those whose eggs reach the bottom broken can expect misfortune.

Divination from onions (cromniomancy)

To answer a question
Decide on the possible answers to your question.
Attach the answers to different onions.
- The answer to your question will be revealed by
  the first onion to sprout.

To make a wish come true
Wish while burning onion skins on a fire.

To find the name of the person you will marry
Attach the names of possible suitors to several
onions. Leave them to sprout.
- The name of your future partner will be revealed by
  the first onion to sprout.

Divination from apples

Wishing on an apple

Cut an apple in half through the center while you
make a wish.
- Your wish will come true if you have cut the apple
  through without cutting any of the pips.

To know the initial of the next person to visit you

Cut an apple into nine pieces. While repeating the
alphabet aloud, throw the last piece over your
shoulder.
- The letter you have reached when the piece of
  apple touches the floor will be the initial of the
  person who will visit you next.

To see your future partner

There are two ways of doing this:
1 Sit alone in front of a mirror on Halloween. Comb
your hair while eating an apple.
- You will see the reflection of your future partner
  looking over your left shoulder.

2 Cut the apple into nine pieces and eat eight with
your back to the mirror. Throw the ninth piece over
your shoulder and turn quickly to look in the glass.
- You should see the reflection of your future partner.

To know when you will marry

A group of people each tie a piece of string to an
apple and whirl them around.
- The apple that falls off the string first indicates the
  person who will marry first.
- Whoever owns the last apple to fall will not marry
  at all.

To know the initial of the name of your future partner

There are two ways to do this:

1 Carefully peel an apple so that the peel remains in one long piece. Count off the twists using letters of the alphabet.

- The last letter you call will be the initial of your future partner.

2 Carefully peel an apple so that the peel remains in one long piece. Throw the peel over your shoulder.

- The initial that the peel resembles when it falls is the initial of your future partner.

Bobbing for apples

There are two methods of bobbing:

1 Put several apples into a bowl of water. A group of people should try and secure an apple in their mouths without using their hands.

- The first person to secure an apple will be the first to marry.
- Prosperity is indicated by the relative size of the apple—the bigger the apple, the more prosperous you will be.

2 Before the apples are put into the bowl, women make secret marks on them and then the men try to seize apples in their mouths without using their hands.

- The apple a man gets indicates the woman he will marry.

An apple breaking as you eat it

- This is considered to be bad luck.

Divination from puddings and cakes

Wedding cake

There are two ways to find who you will marry:

1 Pass a piece of wedding cake three times through a borrowed wedding ring. On a piece of paper, write the name of the person you think you may marry. Wrap the cake in the paper and sleep with it under your pillow.

- You should then dream of your future partner.

2 Fast throughout Friday and then fall asleep with a piece of wedding cake under your pillow.

- You should then dream of your future partner.

Christmas pudding

There are two ways of using Christmas pudding:

1 Before the pudding is cooked, stir into it a small silver coin.

- Prosperity comes to the person who finds the coin in their pudding.

2 Before the pudding is cooked, stir into it a selection of charms.

- Fortune depends on the charm found in the pudding. For example, a ring might indicate a wedding; a horseshoe might indicate luck.

Dumb cake

This form of divination must be carried out in complete silence, on Midsummer's Eve. Three people mix together flour, water and a little sugar for making a cake. Together they knead the ingredients. Once the cake is baked it is broken into three. Each person breaks their third into nine pieces. All pieces are passed through a wedding ring, borrowed from someone who has worn it for at least three years. Each person then eats their nine pieces of cake. The wedding ring is hung over the bed in which they all must sleep.

- Each person will dream of their future partner.

Dreaming bannock

A bannock is a traditional unleavened oatcake. In complete silence, bake a bannock on Shrove Tuesday evening and to the mixture add a silver ring and some small silver charms. Cut the finished bannock into as many pieces as there are unmarried people present.

- Each person's future for the next twelve months will be revealed by the type of charm they find.
- Each person wraps their piece of bannock in a stocking or sock and places it under their pillow.
- They will then dream of their future partner.

Twelfth Night cake

Keep a piece of Twelfth Night cake in a dry place for three months.

- If the cake does not become mouldy, you will enjoy good fortune for the rest of the year.

GEOMANCY

Definition Divination by the earth.

History There are various methods of geomancy: Navajo wise men have allowed sand to trickle through their fingers into prophetic patterns on the ground; Arab geomancers have interpreted the patterns made when a handful of sand or dust is cast onto a smooth surface; and some African witch doctors have read the marks made by a crab scrambling around in a bowl of wet sand.

Modern methods Newer methods of geomancy involve the interpretation of random marks made in sand or on paper with a pointer, a process similar to automatic writing.

Equipment Some earth (such as sand, dust, or dry soil) (**a**) and a pointer (such as a sharp stick or a pencil) (**b**). For paper geomancy you need some paper (**c**) and a pencil (**d**).

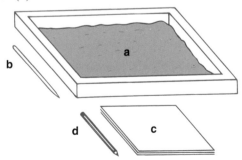

READING THE SAND

You can try geomancy for yourself in the following way:

1 Spread out some fine, dry sand onto a flat space on the ground or onto a tray.

2 Either wear a blindfold or sit in complete darkness.

3 Sit in silence. (If you are attempting to help answer a question for a friend, he or she should sit next to you, concentrating on the question to be answered.)

4 Resting your wrist on the edge of the tray, allow the pointer to lightly touch the sand.

5 Clear all thoughts from your mind. Allow the pointer to move of its own accord.

6 Once you are sure that the pointer has finished moving, inspect the sand.

Reading the marks made in sand

A series of symbols, letters, parts of words, or even complete words may have been formed in the sand. Illustrated here are some possible marks and their meanings.

Mark	Possible meaning
M, m	Maybe
N, n (**a**)	No
P, p	Perhaps
Y, y	Yes
Short, separated lines (**b**)	Lack of purpose
Short, deep line	A visitor
Long, deep line	A journey
Small, scattered crosses	Dissension and conflict
Large cross	Love affair (happy if distinct, unhappy if indistinct)
Small circle	Coming marriage
Large circle	Misfortune at hand
Triangle	Successful career
Square (**c**)	Protection
Birds (**d**)	News, travel
Mountain (**e**)	Fame, a move or change
House	Stability
Sword	Success and peace if pointing upward; failure or illness if pointing downward

It is possible to establish a rough timescale by taking
the whole width of the sand to represent one year,
dividing it into sections for months.

PAPER GEOMANCY

In paper geomancy, the diviner uses a pencil or a pen to make marks onto paper. Dots made on paper are given Latin names which probably date from the thirteenth century.

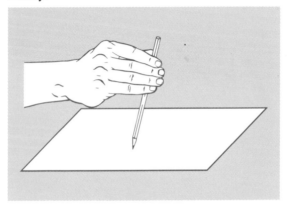

You can try paper geomancy in the following way:

1 Using minimum control over the pencil, make four groups of four rows of random points.

2 Count up the points in each row: an even number in a row is represented by two dots, an odd number by one dot. This converts each group of four rows into one of 16 possible shapes made out of dots.

Some diviners interpret these shapes as they stand. Others manipulate them according to a complex set of rules, translating some shapes into others and interpreting the resulting patterns in light of their relationship with the 12 astrological houses.

Reading dots made on paper

1 **Fortuna major** Great good fortune
2 **Fortuna minor** Less good fortune
3 **Via** Way
4 **Populus** People, nation
5 **Acquisitio** To seek, to gain
6 **Laetitia** Happiness
7 **Amissio** Loss
8 **Puella** Girl
9 **Puer** Boy
10 **Conjunctio** Joining, meeting
11 **Albus** White
12 **Rubeus** Red
13 **Carcer** Prison
14 **Tristitia** Sadness
15 **Caput draconis** Dragon's head
16 **Cauda draconis** Dragon's tail

1
2
3
4
5
6
7
8
9
10
11
12
13
14
15
16

GRAPHOLOGY

Definition Assessing a person's character from their handwriting.

History Graphology is an ancient art: thousands of years ago the Chinese analyzed the characters in their calligraphy; monks in the Middle Ages studied character from handwriting, as had the Romans before them. In 1622 Camillo Baldo, an Italian, wrote what is known to be the oldest surviving treatise on graphology. It was not until the nineteenth and twentieth centuries that graphology began to be viewed as a science rather than an art.

Modern methods Today, graphologists are employed throughout the commercial world by the personnel departments of many large companies. As consultants they are required to help assess existing employees or job applicants. The psychologist Carl Jung was one of the first to realize the significance of handwriting as an aid to understanding character and personality and many universities in the USA, France, Germany, and Israel include graphology in their psychology and criminology courses. Extensive research carried out in the nineteenth and twentieth centuries—mostly by French and German graphologists—forms the basis of many techniques still in use by today's handwriting analysts. The principles of graphology are explained here to enable you to try this form of character assessment for yourself.

Equipment You do not require any special equipment for graphology, just a sample of handwriting.

Basic principles

Although they may be similar, no two handwritings are identical. Each person's handwriting is unique and therefore provides an insight to their individual character. However, it is important when making your analysis that you bear in mind the following points:

● A person's handwriting can vary. Handwriting may be affected by illness or worry, for example, and for this reason it would be unwise to oversimplify your analysis, or to make an analysis based solely on one sample of handwriting.

● Graphology cannot be used to reveal the sex of a person since everyone has a combination of male and female traits in their biological and psychological makeup.

● Graphology cannot be used to identify the age of a person since some people are mature at 25 and others are still young in outlook at 75.

● No single trait can be assessed without taking into account all others.

Aspects of handwriting which must be taken into account include:

● Use of zones
● Use of margins
● Slant of writing
● Pressure used
● Size of writing
● Slope of the baseline
● Spacing of characters
● Connecting strokes
● Starting and ending strokes
● Capitals
● Signatures
● Ink color

ZONES

One of the things to analyze in a sample of handwriting
is the way zones are used. Handwriting can be divided
into three zones: upper, middle, and lower.

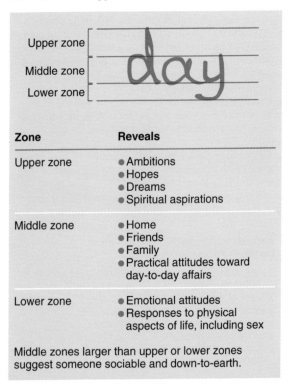

Zone	Reveals
Upper zone	● Ambitions ● Hopes ● Dreams ● Spiritual aspirations
Middle zone	● Home ● Friends ● Family ● Practical attitudes toward day-to-day affairs
Lower zone	● Emotional attitudes ● Responses to physical aspects of life, including sex

Middle zones larger than upper or lower zones
suggest someone sociable and down-to-earth.

Loops

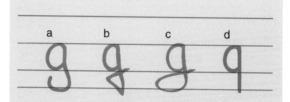

Type	Character
a Long, rounded	A romantic attitude to love and life
b Triangular	A domestic tyrant, or someone who has been disappointed (usually sexually) in his or her partner
c Inflated	Imagination and an exaggerated ego
d Straight	A fatalist with good concentration and an ability to get down to essentials rapidly and without fuss

Upper loops in the letters d, k and l show, according to size and height, the writer's ideals, tendency to daydream, and degree of interest in the spiritual life.

MARGINS

Margins reveal educational and social qualities.

Margin	Character traits
Wide left margin	• Cultural background • Intelligent • Aesthetic sense
Narrow left margin	• Indiscriminate friendliness • Meanness
Wide right margin	• Apprehension about the future
Narrow right margin	• Reserved approach to making friends and to the world in general • Lack of discrimination
Wide upper margin	• Formal and reserved
Wide lower margin	• Fear of sex
Narrow lower margin	• Instinct to hoard • Can be overfamiliar • Lack of reserve

SLANT

Direction of slant	Character traits
To the right *day*	• Extrovert; the greater the slant the more gregarious the writer • Outward-going • Need and capacity for human contact • Desire to give and receive affection
To the left *day*	• Introvert; the greater the slant, the greater the degree of introversion • Guided by the head rather than the heart
Varied *day*	• Versatile personality • Can be unstable • Changeable • Frequently moody—pulled between impulse and control, mind and emotion

PRESSURE

The pressure and thickness of the strokes reveal the
strength of libido and sensual impulse.

Pressure	Character traits
Light *day*	● Sensitive ● Critical ● Lack of vitality (if very light)
Medium *day*	● Average person with average impulses
Heavy *day*	● Sensual ● Energetic

SIZE

Size	Character
Very small	A person with an inferiority complex (if the script dissolves into a line).
Small	An academic who likes to rationalize everything, even emotional behavior. Scientists, researchers and those who deal with ideas fit this category.
Medium	A person who is reasonable and adaptable and able to fit into most surroundings. With a composed attitude, the writer is generally polite and neither too shy nor too bold.
Large	Someone who needs an active social life to be happy; an expansive nature; loves being in the limelight.
Very large	Someone egotistical, perhaps with an overbearing, abrasive nature; monopolizes conversation; dominates the social scene.

BASELINE SLOPE

Slope	Character traits
A steady, firm baseline	Well-balanced; straightforward; moods kept under control; not easily swayed by other people; persevering.
Slopes downward (**a**)	Depressed and pessimistic, increasing with the severity of the slope.
Slopes upward (**b**)	Ambitious and optimistic, increasing with the severity of the slope.
Varying, some lines sloping up, others sloping down	Moody.
Writing changes in terms of both slope and pressure	Allows feelings to brush aside reason; can be impetuous and unreliable.

a *day*   **b** *day*

SPACING

Spacing between words and letters reveals the degree of discrimination a writer has in choosing friends, and how generous or mean they are.

Spacing	Character traits
Narrow spacing between lines	Inability to plan and poor organizational ability.
Wide spacing between lines	The ability to look ahead objectively.
Narrow spacing between words (**a**)	A need for people and for a full social life.
Wide spacing between words (**b**)	Reserve and caution in choosing acquaintances.

a

The cat sat on the mat

b

The   cat   sat   on   the

STARTING AND ENDING STROKES

Starting and ending strokes on letters indicate fussiness and often caution.

Slope	Character traits
Starting strokes (**a**)	A person who is not particularly receptive to new ideas or projects, who prefers to stick to tried and tested methods.
Ending strokes (**b**)	These suggest a reluctance to let go and are found in the writing of the type of person who takes a long time to say goodbye on the telephone.
Writing with no starting or ending strokes	An ability to get down to essentials quickly without wasting time or effort.

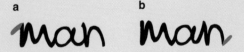

a   b

CONNECTED/DISCONNECTED WRITING

Type	Character traits
Connected handwriting (**a**)	• A logical and systematic thinker • Cooperative and reasonable approach to others • Lacks initiative and intuitive thinking • Unlikely to be spontaneous • May lack originality
Disconnected handwriting (**b**)	• Egotistic • Inconsistent • Obstinate • Brushes aside the ideas of others • Can be moody • Can dislike social intercourse • May produce original and creative ideas

a The cat sat on the mat

b The cat sat on the mat

CONNECTING STROKES

Connecting stroke	Style
ARCADE WRITERS	Have pronounced connection in their archlike script

and one mind

| THREAD WRITERS | Letters are joined together in a threadlike formation |

Here I enclose a

| ANGULAR WRITING | A disciplined movement in the linking of letters |

If I want a

| THE GARLAND | A quick way of joining letters together |

another form

Positive traits	Negative traits
• Appreciate art and have a sense of form and style • Tendency to secretiveness and depth of feeling • Sticklers for formality	• Slightly mistrustful • Affect pretentiousness accompanied by a capacity for intrigue
• Psychologically skilled in dealing with people • Intelligent • Versatile • Highly adaptable • Can be all things to all people	• Can be elusive and hard to pin down • Sometimes deceitful
• Strong willed • Firm • Decisive • Persistent • Have a disciplined attitude to life and love	• May be aggressive • Can be blind to other viewpoints • Lack adaptability • Suspicious • Domineering • Lack empathy
• Easy-going personality • Adaptable • Flexible • Kind • Sympathetic	• Lazy • Easily influenced • Superficial feelings

CAPITALS

These reveal the writer's ego and public face. Some are more significant in graphology than others, although size and shape must be taken into account for them all.

Capital	Character traits
Printed capitals	A sign of literary ability or familiarity with the printed word; usually denote good taste and an ability for constructive planning.
Small or smaller than rest of script	An over-modest attitude; lacks self-assurance and self-confidence
Inflated	A desire to be admired and noticed. Writer may be a conceited person or a leader, or both—or may be compensating for an inferiority complex
Enrolled or scroll-like or with embellishments	Suggests vulgarity
Original or unique	Found in the writing of artists and other creative people

Capital M

This capital provides clues to the writer's ego.

Capital M style	Character traits
Has a higher first stroke (**a**)	Healthy ego
Higher end stroke (**b**)	A cooperative or subordinate personality; someone who heeds public opinion
Large loop on the beginning slope (**c**)	Jealousy
Rounded (**d**)	Non-aggression
Angular (**e**)	Forcefulness and drive, sometimes to the point of selfishness

a *Maybe*   b *Maybe*

c *Maybe*

d *Maybe*   e *Maybe*

Capital I

This is a unique capital because it reveals a writer's self-assessment and motivation.

Capital I style	Character traits
Larger than the other capitals (**a**)	Self-interest; demands attention; self-confidence masks uncertainty
Small and poorly formed (**b**)	Weak willed; self-consciousness
Made to form a circle (**c**)	Introversion and a desire to protect the ego
Huge, inflated and round (**d**)	Egotistic; exaggerated self-importance; must be in the limelight
Small letter used instead of a capital (**e**)	Suggests self-devaluation
Straight line down (**f**)	Sophisticated; a strong ego; unpretentious; intelligent
Made in three parts (**g**)	A fragmented personality
Slants to the left or is upright when rest of writing slants to the right (**h**)	Suggests a guilt complex

It also provides clues to the writer's vanity, and to modesty and unselfishness.

a   I was

b   I have

c   Every Day I

d   I find

e   i was very

f   I was

g   I really

h   I can't

SIGNATURES

These show the facade the writer puts up to the world.

Signature	Character traits
Clearly written and easily understood	Honesty; reliability
Small, compressed, narrow	An inferiority complex
Large and full of flourishes	Lack of taste; an exaggerated ego
Underlined	Egotistical; forceful
Threadlike, tapers off into lines	Calculating; clever; diplomatic; intelligent; often with a capacity for dealing with people
Circle around signature	May be a sign of depression and a cry for help
Lines going through the signature	Lack of ego; self-doubt

INK COLOR

In addition to the style of a person's writing, it is important that graphologists take into account what color ink has been used.

Ink color	Character traits
Black	Conventionally-minded; efficient; cool; someone who wants to impress. More assertive than blue but not as assertive as red
Blue	A happy color suggesting a friendly attitude. Less assertive than black
Red	Favored by those with an exaggerated ego; someone who loves to be the center of attention; sensual. More assertive than either blue or black
Green	Often used by young people who wish to appear different

I CHING

Definition The I Ching—also known as the Book of Changes—is an ancient Chinese text, regarded by many as a book of wisdom. Central to I Ching is the hexagram, a shape made by the questioner (though not a geometric hexagram), and interpreted using the Book of Changes, from which fortune is predicted and advice provided on how to deal with it.

History The I Ching has existed in various forms for the last 4000 years and results from the work of different individuals. The hexagram at the heart of I Ching consists of a pattern of broken and unbroken lines. These have been ascribed to the first Emperor of China, the mythical figure Fu Hsi. Eight shapes—known as trigrams—made by combining the broken and unbroken lines, are said to have been discovered on the shell of an ancient tortoise. Under the Hsia Dynasty (2205–1766 B.C.) two early books of changes were used for divination. The present set of 64 hexagrams is thought to have been compiled by King Wen (died c. 1150 B.C.) who also began adding explanatory text. Wen's son, the Duke of Chou, continued this process to create the oracle that was used throughout the Chou Dynasty (1150–249 B.C.). It is believed that Confucius wrote an additional commentary and, later, the rest were attributed to him as well. The I Ching was submerged in magic and the Yin-Yang doctrine during the Ch'in (221–206 B.C.) and Han (A.D. 206–220) Dynasties and rescued by a scholar called Wang Pi (A.D. 226-249) who argued that it should be used not only as a means of divination, but also as a fund of wisdom.

Modern methods Present texts are based on the early eighteenth century edition of the I Ching called Chou I Che Chung. The most widely used translations in the West are those of James Legge and Richard Wilhelm.

Equipment The information supplied here is intended as an overall guide. For detailed divination you will need to refer to a copy of the actual I Ching, in one of the English translations. To construct the hexagram shape you will need coins or plant stalks (traditionally yarrow stalks).

Lines

Hexagrams are made from trigrams, which are themselves constructed from a combination of two types of line: unbroken and broken.

The unbroken line (a)
Now called Yang, heaven, or "the firm," this began as a simple sign for "yes" in divination. It is associated with the positive, active, and masculine side of nature.

The broken line (b)
Now called Yin, earth, "the yielding," this began as a sign for "no," and represents the negative, feminine, passive side of nature.

Trigrams: construction

Hexagrams are made from trigrams, each of which combines the two types of line—unbroken and broken—in a different way. The lines are grouped in threes, in every possible combination, producing eight trigrams in all. These are read from the bottom up, line by line, and are shown here along with their Chinese characters. Trigrams are considered symbols of change, one constantly changing into another. Each type of line has special significance according to its position in the trigram.

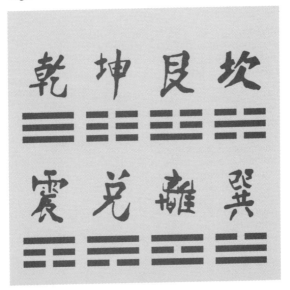

Trigrams

Trigrams each have a name, an attribute, an image and a family relationship. These are shown on the next four pages.

Names

The Chinese names given to each trigram do not appear anywhere else in the Chinese language. English translations are not always agreed upon and the Wade system of spelling which has been used in our translations is now officially obsolete—but is still found in most editions of the I Ching.

Attributes

These refer to the kind of action that is latent in the trigram.

Images

Associated images represent ideas that can add depth to the interpretation of that trigram when it is found as part of a hexagram.

Family relationships

The relationships listed on the following pages are those given by King Wen. Daughters are usually associated with devotion; sons with movement.

Some authors link trigrams to even more themes, such as points of the compass, parts of the body, animals, and time of day.

Trigrams (continued)

Trigram	Chinese name	Name Translated
	Ch'ien	The creative
	K'un	The receptive
	Chen	The arousing
	K'an	The abysmal

Attribute	Image relationship	Family
Strong	Heaven	Father
Devoted, yielding	Earth	Mother
Inciting movement	Thunder	First son
Dangerous	Water	Second son

(continued)

Trigrams (continued)

Trigram	Chinese name	Name Translated
	Ken	Keeping still
	Sun	The gentle
	Li	The clinging
	Tui	The joyous

Attribute	Image relationship	Family
Resting	Mountain	Third son
Penetrating	Wind, wood	First daughter
Light-giving	Fire	Second daughter
Joyful	Lake	Third daughter

Hexagrams

Using the eight trigrams, King Wen devised 64
hexagrams, each of which was given a name and a
number. Each of the 64 hexagrams was formed by
combining two trigrams.

The sovereign hexagrams

Twelve of the 64 hexagrams represent the twelve lunar
months of the Chinese year (shown below) and reflect
the rise and fall of Yang and Yin throughout the
seasons. For this reason they are thought to be
particularly significant.

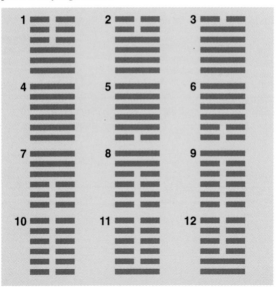

Identifying a hexagram

When you begin casting your own hexagrams, it is useful to use the table provided (overleaf) to identify which hexagram you have cast.

1 Divide the hexagram in half to produce two trigrams.
2 Using the table shown on the next two pages, look up the lower trigram in the left hand column of the table.
3 Look up the upper trigram in the upper row of the table.
4 Read across from the lower trigram, and down from the upper trigram, and the box at which the two meet is your hexagram.

Example:
The lower part of the hexagram is Li (**a**) and the upper part is Ken (**b**). Refer to the table shown on the next two pages. Reading across for Li and down for Ken we find the hexagram Pi, number 22.

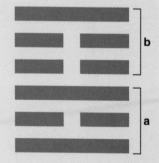

Hexagram identification

UPPER TRIGRAM LOWER TRIGRAM	Ch'ien	Chen	K'an	Ken
Ch'ien	Ch'ien 1	Ta Chuang 34	Hsu 5	Ta Ch'u 26
Chen	Wu Wang 25	Chen 51	Chun 3	I 27
K'an	Sung 6	Chieh 40	K'an 29	Meng 4
Ken	Tun 33	Hsiao Kuo 62	Chien 39	Ken 52
K'un	P'i 12	Yu 16	Pi 8	Po 23
Sun	Kou 44	Heng 32	Ching 48	Ku 18
Li	T'ing Jen 13	Feng 55	Chi Chi 63	Pi 22
Tui	Lu 10	Kuei Mei 54	Chien 60	Sun 41

K'un	Sun	Li	Tui
T'ai	Hsiao Ch'u	Ta Yu	Kuai
11	9	14	43
Fu	I	Shih Ho	Sui
24	42	21	17
Shih	Huan	Wei Chi	K'un
7	59	64	47
Ch'ien	Chien	Lu	Hsien
15	53	56	31
K'un	Kuan	Chin	Ts'ui
2	20	35	45
Sheng	Sun	Ting	Ta Kuo
46	57	50	28
Ming I	Chia Jen	Li	Ko
36	37	30	49
Lin	Chung Fu	K'uei	Tui
19	61	38	58

Complete list of hexagrams

Number	Chinese name	Translated name
1	Ch'ien	The creative
2	K'un	The receptive
3	Chun	Difficulty at the beginning
4	Meng	Youthful folly
5	Hsu	Waiting
6	Sung	Conflict
7	Shih	The army
8	Pi	Holding together
9	Hsiao Ch'u	The taming power of the small
10	Lu	Treading
11	T'ai	Peace
12	P'i	Standstill
13	T'ung Jen	Fellowship with men
14	Ta Yu	Possession in great measure
15	Ch'ien	Modesty
16	Yu	Enthusiasm
17	Sui	Following
18	Ku	Work on what has been spoiled
19	Lin	Approach
20	Kuan	Contemplation
21	Shih Ho	Biting through

Number	Chinese name	Translated name
22	Pi	Grace
23	Po	Splitting apart
24	Fu	Return
25	Wu Wang	Innocence
26	Ta Ch'u	The taming power of the great
27	I	The corners of the mouth
28	Ta Kuo	Preponderance of the great
29	K'an	The abysmal
30	Li	The clinging
31	Hsien	Influence
32	Heng	Duration
33	Tun	Retreat
34	Ta Chuang	The power of the great
35	Chin	Progress
36	Ming I	Darkening of the light
37	Chia Den	The family
38	K'uei	Opposition
39	Chien	Obstruction
40	Hsieh	Deliverance
41	Sun	Decrease

continued

Complete list of hexagrams (continued)

Number	Chinese name	Translated name
42	I	Increase
43	Kuai	Breakthrough
44	Kou	Coming to meet
45	Ts'ui	Gathering together
46	Sheng	Pushing upward
47	K'un	Oppression
48	Ching	The well
49	Ko	Revolution
50	Ting	The caldron
51	Chen	The arousing
52	Ken	Keeping still
53	Chien	Development
54	Kuei Mei	The marrying maiden
55	Feng	Abundance
56	Lu	The wanderer
57	Sun	The gentle
58	Tui	The joyous
59	Huan	Dispersion
60	Chieh	Limitation
61	Chung Fu	Inner truth
62	Hsiao Kuo	Preponderance of the small
63	Chi Chi	After completion
64	Wei Chi	Before completion

Strong lines

Both types of line—unbroken (Yang) and broken (Yin)—can be strong. A strong Yang line has a circle over the center (**a**) and a strong Yin line has a cross in the gap (**b**).

a   **b**

If your hexagram contains one of these lines:
1 Interpret the hexagram as it stands,
2 Convert the lines to their opposites: a strong Yang becomes a Yin and a strong Yin becomes a Yang.
3 Interpret the hexagram with these new lines.

Example:
This hexagram is P'i number 12 (**c**), made up of a lower trigram, K'un, number 2; and an upper trigram, Ch'ien, number 1. When the strong lines are reversed, the hexagram becomes K'uei (**d**), number 38, made up of a lower trigram Tui number 58, and an upper trigram, Li, number 30.

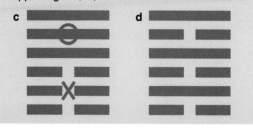

CASTING

Hexagrams are formed by casting, using either coins or
traditional yarrow sticks. Although both methods are
adequate, some prefer to use the yarrow sticks as the
process is far lengthier than using coins, and this is
thought to concentrate the mind more.

Casting using coins

For this you will need three old Chinese coins (**a**).
Round, with a hole in the center, they have characters
on one side only. Alternatively you can improvise using
standard coins.

a

1 Give the side with characters a value of two. If using
  standard coins this is the side with the monetary value
  on it.
2 The plain side is given a value of three. For standard
  coins this is the side without monetary value.

3 Shake all three coins together in your hands and then drop them onto a flat surface.

4 Add together the value of the uppermost sides and write it down. It will be either 6, 7, 8, or 9. (Remember that the value of a side with characters is two, and the value of a plain side is three). For example:

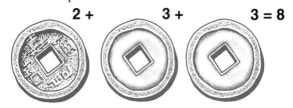

2 +   **3 +**   **3 = 8**

5 Throw the coins five more times and each time add up the total of the uppermost faces and write it above the last total. You should have thrown the coins six times in all, and have six numbers, one for each time the coins were thrown.

6 Convert the six numbers to Yang or Yin lines, using the key below. Note that 6 is a strong Yin line and 9 is a strong Yang line.

Converting totals to either Yang or Yin lines

Total	Line		Total	Line
6 =	━━━✕━━━		**8** =	━━━ ━━━
7 =	━━━━━━		**9** =	━━━◯━━━

Example: casting a hexagram using coins

Throw	Coins	Total value	Line
sixth		= 8	▬▬ ▬▬
fifth		= 8	▬▬ ▬▬
fourth		= 7	▬▬▬▬▬
third		= 6	▬▬✕▬▬
second		= 9	▬▬◯▬▬
first		= 9	▬▬◯▬▬

The resulting hexagram is Kuei Mei 54 (**a**), made from a lower trigram, Tui 58, and an upper trigram, Chen 51. When the strong lines are converted to their opposites, this hexagram becomes Hsiao Kuo 62 (**b**), made up from a lower trigram, Ken 52, and an upper trigram, Chen 51.

(**a**) Kuei Mei (**b**) Hsiao Kuo

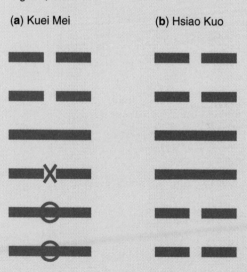

Both hexagrams need to be looked up in the book of I Ching.

Casting using yarrow stalks
This is a much more lengthy method of casting
hexagrams than using coins, and is favored by some
diviners. You will need 49 yarrow stalks—a plant
traditionally associated with Chinese divination—
although specially prepared strips of bamboo can also
be bought.

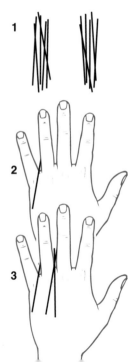

1 Working on a flat
surface, divide your
stalks arbitrarily into
two piles.

2 Using your right hand,
take a stalk from the right-
hand pile and place it
between little finger and
ring finger of your left
hand.

3 Using your right hand,
discard stalks from the
left-hand pile, four at a
time, until four, three,
two or one remain. Place
the remaining stalks
between the middle
fingers of your left hand.

4 Using your right hand, reduce the right-hand pile four at a time until four or fewer stalks remain. Put these between the middle and index fingers of your left hand.

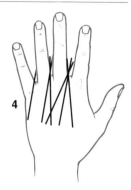

5 Put all the stalks form your left hand carefully to one side.

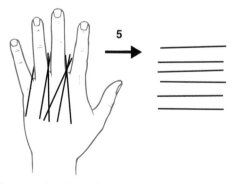

6 Heap together the stalks that were discarded four at a time.

7 Repeat the entire procedure twice more.

8 When you have carried out this procedure three times you will have three groups of stalks, set aside each time you reached stage five. Add these together. You will find that they total 13, 17, 21, or 25.

9 Using the table here, convert your number to a Yin, Yang, strong Yin or strong Yang.

10 The type of line indicated by the number becomes the bottom line of your hexagram.

11 Repeat this process for each of the remaining five lines of your hexagram.

CONSULTING THE I CHING

Perhaps the hardest part about this form of divination is in consulting the I Ching once you have obtained your hexagram. Some people prefer to pay for the services of a professional reader as the text is cryptic and difficult to follow. Here we provide just a brief guidance to some of the more obscure expressions you might come across and the parts into which the text is divided.

How the text is organized

When you consult the I Ching you may find up to five entries for your hexagram, although this varies with different editions of the text.

Section	Description
The Judgment (or decision)	Said to have been composed by King Wen, this section describes the essence of the situation.
The commentary on the judgment	This section is self-explanatory. It is Confucian or post-Confucian in origin.
The image (or symbol)	This section takes the judgment a stage further by supplying images that link it with the human sphere. It is also attributed to King Wen.
The lines	These interpretations of the strong or moving lines were made by the Duke of Chou, King Wen's son. Although explicit in offering advice, they do not refer to the weak or normal lines.

Ways of reading hexagrams

Bottom up
You read a hexagram by starting with the line at the bottom and working upward. Lines are numbered 1–6 for reference only.

6
5
4
3
2
1

Pairs of lines
Each hexagram can be divided into pairs of lines. The lower (**a**) refers to earth, the middle (**b**) to man, and the upper (**c**) to heaven.

c
b
a

Primary trigrams
Hexagrams are composed of two trigrams. These are referred to as the lower (**a**) and upper (**b**) primary trigrams.

b

a

Nuclear trigrams
Within each hexagram are two trigrams interlocked. These are known as the lower (**a**) and upper (**b**) nuclear trigrams.

b
a

Some common expressions explained

Expression	Explanation
Correct	Refers to a Yang line in first, third, or fifth place; a Yin line in second, fourth or sixth place.
Inner	The lower primary trigram.
Outer	The upper primary trigram.
Movement	Associated with Yang.
No blame/no error	You can correct your course without incurring permanent harm.
Supreme success	The most favorable indication that you are on the correct course of action.
The superior man/ great man/sage	The paragon of correct behavior, fully in accord with the doctrine of Tao.
Misfortune	A mild indication that your course is wrong.
Peril	An intermediate warning of a dangerous course, between evil and misfortune.
Evil	The strongest indication of a dangerous course.

METOPOSCOPY

Definition Method of assessing character and fortune from lines on the forehead. The term metoposcopy is derived from the Greek, *metopon*, meaning forehead.
History The development of metoposcopy is usually credited to an Italian, Geronimo or Gerolamo Cardano (1501–1576), otherwise known as Jerome Cardan. An eminent physician, physicist, mathematician and

Reading forehead lines

Line	Fortune
Wavy line	Travel by sea. If turning down at both ends, travel on land; if turning up at both ends, travel by air
Straight line curved at one end	Ill health
Slightly tilted line	Happiness
One horizontal line	Success in war
One diagonal line	Adventure
Two well-spaced horizontal lines	Happiness, good fortune
Three horizontal lines placed high on forehead	Gentle, peaceful, financially unstable
Three horizontal lines placed low on forehead	Aggressive

astrologer, Cardan combined his knowledge of astrology with his observations of several hundred faces to arrive at his theory that character could be read in the lines of the forehead.

Modern methods The method of metoposcopy has remained unchanged for centuries. The forehead is divided into equidistant parallel strips. These strips allow the reader to establish which of the planet lines are present, and to interpret them.

Equipment No equipment is needed.

Line	Fortune
Three well-spaced horizontal lines	Intelligent, kind, good, religious
Three horizontal lines cut by a vertical line	Longevity
Line running close to hairline	If complete, intelligence; if broken, irritability
Line over left eyebrow	Imaginative
Line over right eyebrow	Ambition. If long, success; if broken, egotistic
Vertical lines between eyebrows	One line, singleminded; two lines, changeable; three lines, practical; four lines, active mind, involved in a wide range of activities

Reading planetary lines

Line	Meaning
1 Line of Saturn	If straight and well-defined: caution, intelligence, perception, discernment
2 Line of Jupiter	If straight and well-defined: integrity, magnanimity, good fortune; if longer than the line of Saturn: riches
3 Line of Mars	If deeply etched: courage, ambition, endurance; if broken: argumentative, self-indulgent
4 Line of the Sun	If straight and well-defined: ambition, worldly success; if broken: egotism, greed; if curved: malevolence; if crossed by another line: honor, acclaim, wealth

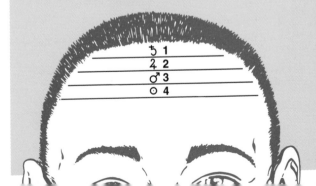

Line	Meaning
5 Line of Venus	If clear: happiness in love; if broken: a series of romances
6 Line of Mercury	If curved upward: good luck; if divided into three: humor, eloquence
7 Line of the Moon	If clear: travel, imagination, intuition; if broken: temperamental; if crossed by another line: good fortune in times of war

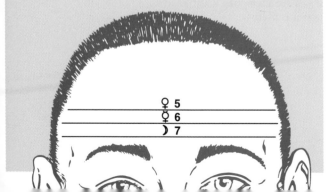

MOLEOSCOPY

Definition Assessing character and fortune from moles on the body.

History Since the time of the ancient Greeks, moles have been considered to be significant indicators of character and fortune. Moleoscopy reached the height of its popularity during the sixteenth and seventeenth centuries, when elaborate treatises linked the relative position of moles on the body with the horoscope. Each part of the body was considered to be ruled by a specific sign of the zodiac and each part of the face by a specific planet, making the position of moles of great astronomical significance.

Modern methods The process of moleoscopy is today much simplified, and does not require the use of complex charts.

Equipment No special equipment is needed. However, if you are attempting a self-analysis, a full-length mirror is useful.

Characteristics of moles

Characteristics	Character and fortune
Honey-colored	Good fortune
Red	Fortunate
Black	Trouble, disappointment
Becoming lighter	Luck improving
Becoming darker	Trouble, disappointment
Changes (e.g. bleeding)	Possible ill health; consult your doctor
Round	Good character
Angular	Bad character
Oval	Bad luck
Oblong	Great prosperity
Raised	Great good fortune
Two moles close together	Two marriages or serious love affairs
Two moles on opposite sides of the body, balancing each other	A dual nature, one side of the character fighting the other

Moles on the face

Position	Character and fortune
Middle of forehead	Bad tempered, can be cruel. Should guard against accidents in middle age
Left temple	Spendthrift, headstrong. Should try to live a quiet life
Right temple	Exceptionally able. Should guard against illness in later life
Eyebrow	Persevering, happy in marriage. Should beware of lightning and food poisoning
Outside corner eye	Honest, forthright, needs to be loved
Ear	Wealth, fame, recklessness
Left cheek	Serious, studious, struggling
Right cheek	Successful life
One on each cheek	Success after a hard struggle
Bridge of nose	Lust, extravagance

Position	Character and fortune
Left side of nose	Changeable, untrustworthy, lucky. Should beware of falls
Right side of nose	Great traveler, needs an outdoor occupation involving plenty of movement
Tip of nose	A sincere friend
Nostrils	A rover
Lips	Greedy but benevolent
Lower lip	Quiet and studious, more fortunate in later life
Chin	Conscientious, has common sense and artistic ability. Makes the best of any opportunities, and improves with age
Left lower jaw	Critical, should beware of ill health
Right lower jaw	Should beware of danger from fire or water

Moles on the body

Position	Character and fortune
1 Throat	An artistic temperament, successful
2 Chest	Lazy, unsteady, quarrelsome, financially unsound
3 Right breast	Indolent, intemperate
4 Left breast	Active, energetic
5 Nipple	Fickle, unfaithful
6 Right ribs	Insensitive, cowardly
7 Left ribs	Lazy, humorous
8 Navel	Great good fortune
9 Abdomen	Voracious, intemperate, self-indulgent. Should marry someone placid
10 Hips	Resourceful, valiant, over-amorous
11 Loins	Mendacious
12 Right thigh	Wealth, a happy marriage
13 Left thigh	A warm temperament

continued

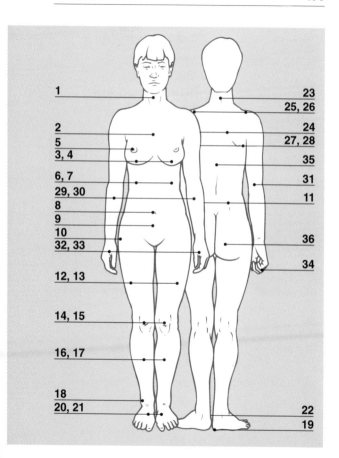

Moles on the body (continued)

Position	Character and fortune
14 Right knee	A friendly disposition, a happy marriage
15 Left knee	Rash, extravagant, ill-tempered, with a good business sense
16 Right leg	Energetic and persevering
17 Left leg	Lazy
18 Ankle	A sharing nature, a sense of humor
19 Heel	Mentally and physically active. Should beware of making enemies
20 Right foot.	Loves traveling
21 Left foot	Thoughtful, gloomy, prefers a sedentary life
22 Instep	Athletic, quarrelsome
23 Neck	Many ups and downs. Should be frugal
24 Shoulder blades	Restrictions, unhappiness
25 Left shoulder	Satisfied with anything

Position	Character and fortune
26 Right shoulder	Prudent, discreet, faithful, restless
27 Left armpit	Good fortune won by hard work
28 Right armpit	Heavy struggles against heavy odds
29 Right arm	Adversity in early life, contentment in old age
30 Left arm	Courteous, industrious
31 Elbow	Great talent, great desire to travel
32 Right wrist of hand	Frugal, successful in business
33 Left wrist or hand	Ingenious, artistic disposition
34 Finger	Dishonest, prone to exaggerate, unable to face reality
35 Back	Frank, with an enquiring mind. Should be cautious
36 Buttocks	Total lack of ambition

NECROMANCY

Definition Asking the dead to answer questions about the future. Replies are transmitted either through a medium at a séance, through automatic writing, or via the mechanical methods of the planchette and ouija board.

History At one time, necromancy involved reanimating a dead body and attempting to get it to answer the questions of the living. The planchette was known to the Chinese and the ouija board was invented in the late nineteenth century by an American, William Fuld.

Planchette

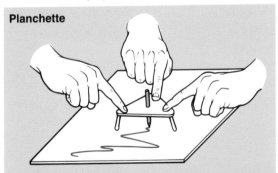

This is a small board, less than six inches long, usually heart-shaped or triangular. A small hole in the planchette is used to hold either a pencil or pointer (for use with ouija boards). Mounted on felt pads, castors or small wheels it can move around freely, about an inch from the table.

Modern methods Automatic writing and use of planchettes and ouija boards are all still in use today. Many spiritualists use séances to try to contact the dead. Many believe that necromancy is best left in the hands of experts and should only be performed under controlled conditions.

Equipment Equipment needed depends on which type of necromancy you are going to try. For automatic writing you require only a pen and some paper. The planchette is a way of stimulating automatic writing using more than one person. With a ouija board, words are spelled out slowly using letters of the alphabet.

Ouija board

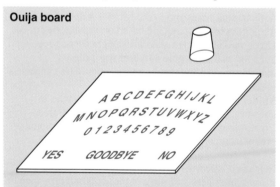

This is made of smooth, polished wood and has the letters of the alphabet on it. Also present are the words "yes," "no," "Goodbye," and numbers 1 to 9. A planchette is used as a pointer, or an upturned glass.

NUMEROLOGY

Definition Form of divination in which numbers exert an influence on every facet of our lives and personality. Also known as numeromancy or arithomancy.

History The Babylonians, ancient Egyptians, and many other peoples are thought to have held theories of the occult significance of numbers. A magico-philosophical science of numbers known as *gematria* is found in the Cabala, the secret and mystical lore of the Jews, and is based on the 22 letters of the Hebrew alphabet. Numbers were especially important to the Cabalists in both ancient times and in the Middle Ages. Most numerological systems are based on the theories of the Greek mathematician and philosopher Pythagoras, who believed that the whole universe was ordered mathematically and that everything could be expressed in terms of numbers.

Modern methods Modern numerologists tend to concentrate on character analysis and potential.

Equipment You do not need any special equipment to practice numerology.

Primary numbers

Primary numbers 1 to 9 are of particular significance to all numerologists and form the basis of all numerological systems. All numbers can be reduced to primary numbers, and it is often necessary to do this when using numerology to assess character.

Reducing any number to its primary
Example: number 32 is reduced to the prime number
5 (3+2=5)

Example: the number 146 is reduced to the primary
2 (1+4+6=11; 1+1 = 2).

Dates are reduced to primary numbers in this way, as can be words, the letters of which are assigned numbers before being added together.

Birth numbers

The birth number is your most important number because it is unchangeable and shows the numerical influence at birth. You can calculate it by adding up the numbers in the date of your birth.

Calculating your birth number
Example: For someone born on February 14, 1954, add 2 (because February is the second month).

$$1+4+1+9+5+4+2 = 26$$

$$2+6 = 8$$

8 is the birth number for this person.

Once you have found your birth number, look up your natural characteristics and basic personality traits from the tables provided.

Name numbers

Name numbers show acquired or developed traits and can be changed.

Calculating your name number

Convert the name you usually use to numbers, using the number-letter equivalents chart below. Add up the numbers in the same way you would for calculating a birth number.

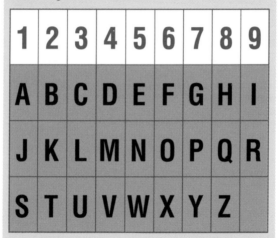

1	2	3	4	5	6	7	8	9
A	B	C	D	E	F	G	H	I
J	K	L	M	N	O	P	Q	R
S	T	U	V	W	X	Y	Z	

Example: Jo Green

j=1, o=6, g=7, r=9, e=5, e=5, n=5

1+6+7+9+5+5+5 = 38; 3+8 =11; 1+1 =2

Numerological analysis

1 Begin your analysis with the birth number. It is known as the "number of personality" and represents your subject's inborn characteristics.

2 Analyze the name number. This is known as the "number of development" and shows traits developed during life. If your subject uses another name at work, or is known by initials, calculate this also. This is known as the "number of attainment" and shows your subject's achievements.

3 Calculate the vowel number. Add up the number equivalents of vowels in your subject's name and reduce them to the primary number. This number is known as the "number of underlying influence."

4 Calculate the frequency number. Take into account any number that occurs frequently when you are calculating birth, name and vowel numbers. This is known as the "number of added influence" and has a modifying effect on the analysis.

Comparing birth and name numbers

It is considered ideal for a person's birth and name numbers to coincide as this will reinforce the characteristics of the birth number. A serious mismatch between the two numbers indicates inner conflicts that remain unresolved.

Using numbers for prediction

You can use numbers for prediction in a variety of ways. For example, if you have an important meeting to go to, add the date on which the meeting is to be held, with your birth number and name number. Interpret your answer.

1

Symbol: the Sun
Day: Sunday
Characteristics: With strength, individuality, and creativity, these people are born leaders, ambitious, active, often aggressive. One is the number of innovators, leaders, winners, but also of tyrants.
Negative qualities: Number 1 people can be self-centered, ruthless and stubborn if crossed.
Relationships: Number 1s will probably put more energy and attention into their chosen career than into their personal relationships.

2

Symbol: the Moon
Day: Monday
Characteristics: Gentle, passive and creative, these people are geared more to thought than to action. They are inventive but less forceful in carrying out their plans than number 1 people. They are likely to have charm and intuition.
Negative qualities: Lack of self-confidence. Can be changeable—even deceitful—as well as over-sensitive and depressive.
Relationships: They get on well with their opposites, the number 1 people.

3

Symbol: Jupiter
Day: Thursday
Characteristics: Energetic, disciplined, talented, these people are also conscientious, proud, and independent. Number 3 is the symbol of the Trinity and a superficial show may hide considerable spirituality.
Negative qualities: Number 3s love to be in control and may be too fond of telling other people what to do.
Relationships: They get on well with other 3s, and those born under 6 and 9.

4

Symbol: Uranus
Day: Sunday
Characteristics: Steady, practical, and with great endurance, these people are seldom interested in material things.
Negative qualities: Number 4—the square—contains its own opposite, and number 4 people often see things from the opposite point of view, making them rebellious and unconventional.
Relationships: Number 4s get on well with people whose number are 1, 2, 7, and 8, but making friends is hard and number 4s may feel isolated.

5

Symbol: Mercury
Day: Wednesday
Characteristics: Lively, sensual, pleasure-seeking, impulsive, and quick-thinking, these people are good at making money, especially by risk or speculation, and they bounce back easily from failure.
Negative qualities: Quick-tempered and highly strung, number 5s may have trouble with their nerves.
Relationships: Number 5s get on well with any number, but especially fellow number 5s.

6

Symbol: Venus
Day: Friday
Characteristics: Love of family and domesticity these people are realiable, trustworthy, and romantic rather than sensual. They have a great love of beauty and are usually attractive. Dislike discord.
Negative qualities: May be obstinate.
Relationships: Number 6s get on well with any number.

7 Ψ

Symbol: Neptune
Day: Monday
Characteristics: Original thinkers who are philosophical and spiritual, and not usually interested in material things. May be highly intuitive, even psychic. Often have a restless love of travel and the sea.
Negative qualities: Have a tendency to become too introverted.
Relationships: May exert an influence on others.

8 ♄

Symbol: Saturn
Day: Saturday
Characteristics: Incorporates the rebellious contradictions of number 4 symbolized by willpower and individuality. May mean sorrow yet is also associated with worldly success. These people have deep and intense feelings.
Negative qualities: May appear cold.
Relationships: Are often misunderstood by others.

9

Symbol: Mars
Day: Tuesday
Characteristics: Fighters, active, and determined, these people usually succeed after a struggle.
Negative qualities: Prone to accident and injury; may be quarrelsome.
Relationships: Highly couragous, demonstrating brotherly love.

♂

Secondary numbers

In addition to the nine primary numbers, secondary numbers are taken into account by some numerologists, but usually only as additional information. Suppose, for example, that a person's birth number and name number are both 12. Both the birth number and name number will be 3 (1+2), but the occurrence of the number 12 for both results suggests that this number has special significance. Some numerologists have created a list of meanings for vast numbers of secondary numbers; others recognize only the secondary numbers up to 22 (note, there are 22 letters in the Hebrew alphabet). The secondary numbers most commonly thought to have significance are 11, 12, 13, 22 and 40.

11 The number of special mystical awareness, possibly balanced between good and evil.

12 A powerful sign of completeness, being the number of the signs of the zodiac, the months, the apostles, etc.

13 One more than the "perfect 12," this number is usually associated with ill fortune and the black arts, but it can also be a positive force.

22 This number has a strong sense of fullness and completeness. It is the number of letters in the Hebrew alphabet, and of cards in the major arcana of the tarot.

40 Another potent number suggesting completeness.

OMENS AND SUPERSTITIONS

Definition Fortune-telling based on traditional beliefs about a wide variety of, for example, animals, plants and objects. Superstitions based on certain objects are often referred to with special names. Lychnomancy, for example, is the name given to divination using three candles; arachnomancy is divination from the appearance of spiders.

History At one time it was the responsibility of augurs and soothsayers to interpret what was considered to be signs sent from the gods. Eventually, the predictions made by soothsayers and the like became common knowledge and passed into folklore.

Modern methods Omens have been known since ancient times and are today referred to as superstitions. They vary among countries and can often have completely reversed meanings.

Equipment Equipment is only needed for specialist types of prediction: an oil lamp is needed for lampadomancy; candles are required for lychnomancy; and a candle plus some precious stones are needed for lithomancy.

SPIDERS (ARACHNOMANCY)

Seeing a spider	Prediction
In the morning	Grief
At noon	Anxiety
In the evening	Financial loss
Spinning a web	Either, there is a plot against you, or you will receive a gift, probably new clothes
Spinning in the morning	Good luck
Spinning in the afternoon	A journey
Climbing its thread	Good news
Dropping on its thread	Good luck, unless it reaches the floor, when it is bad luck
Cross a wall	Good luck
On your clothes	Money, a letter, or both
On your body	Good fortune
A web in a doorway	A visitor
That is small and red	Money
Killing a spider	Bad luck

CATS (AILUROMANCY)

Cat behavior	Prediction
Washing its face or ears	Rain
Climbing the furniture	Rain
Sleeping with its back to the fire	Rain
Following you	Money
Unaccountably leaves home	Disaster
Washing one ear three times	Expect visitors from the direction in which the cat is looking
Sneezing on the day before a wedding	Unlucky for the bride in the USA; lucky elsewhere
Appearing around a door	Think of a question and call for your cat. If its right paw appears first around the door, the answer to your question is yes; if the left paw is first, the answer is no

Cat color	Prediction
A black cat entering your house	Good luck
A black cat crossing your path	Lucky in Britain; unlucky in the USA and some European countries
A black cat walking under a ladder	Bad luck for the next person to climb the ladder
Meeting three black cats in succession	Good luck
A white cat crossing your path	Illness
A gray cat	Good luck

ITCHES

Place of itch	Prediction
1 Top of head	Promotion, good luck
2 Right eye	A meeting
3 Left eye	Disappointment
4 Left cheek or left ear	Compliments
5 Right cheek or right ear	Derogatory remarks
6 Inside nose	Grief, bad luck
7 Outside nose	"Crossed, vexed, or kissed by a fool"
8 Mouth	Insults
9 Neck	Illness
10 Back	Disappointment
11 Left shoulder	Unhappiness
12 Right shoulder	An inheritance
13 Left elbow	Bad news
14 Right elbow	Good news
15 Left palm or ankle	Bills to pay
16 Right palm or ankle	Expect money
17 Abdomen	An invitation
18 Loins	A reconciliation
19 Thighs	A move
20 Left knee	Gossip
21 Right knee	Good news
22 Shins	Unpleasant surprize
23 Left foot	An unprofitable journey
24 Right foot	A profitable journey

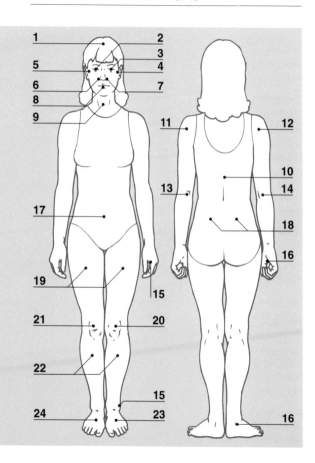

KNIVES AND SCISSORS

Knife/scissors	Prediction
Dropping a knife on the floor	A male visitor
Dropping a pair of scissors	A disappointment, which can be averted by stepping on the scissors before picking them up
Scissors landing point down when dropped	Illness
Crossed knives	Bad luck
Breaking a pair of scissors	Bad luck
A knife left blade upward	Danger
Giving a gift of a knife or scissors	Can cut a friendship unless a pin or a penny is given in exchange
A new knife used first on anything other than paper or wood	Good luck
Placing or finding a knife in the cradle of a newborn child	Good luck

LITHOMANCY

This is divination using precious stones (although colored glass beads can be used as an alternative). In a darkened room, scatter the stones or beads. Light a candle, close your eyes and clear all thoughts from your mind. As soon as you open your eyes, notice which color of stone first reflects the light back at you.

Color	Prediction
Colorless	Success and happiness
Red	Romance
Dark red	A wedding
Yellow	Infidelity
Green	A wish will come true
Turquoise	An unexpected opportunity
Blue	Good luck
Violet	Grief
Purple	A quarrel
Black	Ill luck

LYCHNOMANCY

This is divination from the flames of three wax candles.
Arrange three candles in an equilateral triangle and
light a forth candle some distance away to provide
enough light for the reading. Switch off all other lights.
Using the same match, light your three candles and read
the omens represented by the appearance of their
flames.

Flame	Prediction
A flame wavering from side to side	Travel
One flame burning brighter than the others	Great success
A glow or radiance at the tip of the wick	Prosperity
A curling or spiraling flame	Enemies plotting
Sparks	Be cautious
Rising and falling flames, or candles burning unevenly	Danger
Flame spluttering	Disappointment
Flame unexpectedly extinguished	Great misfortune

LAMPADOMANCY

This is divination using a single oil lamp or a torch flame.

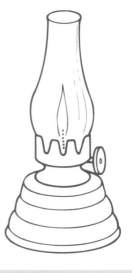

Flame	Prediction
With a single point	Good luck
With two points	Bad luck
With three points	Good luck
Bending	Illness
Unexpectedly extinguished	Disaster

OTHER CANDLE OMENS

To know your luck for the coming year
For this you will need 12 candles and a room with a
wooden or concrete floor.
1 Remove any furnishings that might catch fire.
2 Next, arrange your 12 candles in a circle and light
them all.
3 For each month of the year, name a candle in turn.
4 Start at the January candle and jump over each in
turn until you have been right round the circle.
● If you knock over or extinguish any candle, this
signifies bad luck for that particular month.
● Any candles still burning after you have completed
your circuit indicate good luck for those months
that the candles represent.

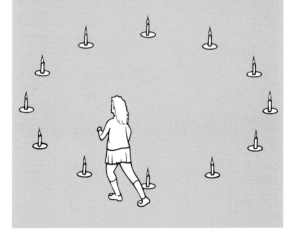

To know if your lover is true

For this you will need a bowl of water, a walnut shell, and two small candles or wax matches.

1 Using a little melted wax to fix them in place, stand one candle in each half of the walnut shell.

2 Name one shell for yourself, the other for your lover.

3 Set the walnut shell boats afloat in the bowl of water.

4 Light the candles.

● You will be true to each other if the two boats float side by side with the candles burning evenly.

● Your relationship is doomed if the boats drift apart, overturn, or the flames go out.

● You love more than you are loved if your candle burns longer than that of your lover, and vice versa.

OMENS OF GOOD LUCK

- A four-leaved clover (**a**).
- Meeting sheep (**b**).
- A ladybug (**c**).
- A horseshoe (**d**).
- A wishbone (**e**).
- Bats flying at twilight (**f**).
- Walking in the rain (**g**).
- A gift of a hive of bees (**h**).
- A peapod containing nine peas (**i**).
- A robin flying into the house.
- Hearing crickets singing.
- A white butterfly.
- Burning your fingernail parings.
- Cutting your hair during a storm.
- Finding a hairpin and hanging it on a hook.
- Seeing a load of hay.
- Looking at the new moon over your right shoulder.
- Picking up a nail that was pointing toward you.
- Picking up a pencil found in the street.
- Keeping a piece of oyster shell in your pocket.
- Carrying a rabbit's foot.
- Sleeping on unironed sheets.
- Spilling your drink while proposing a toast.
- Breaking uncolored glass other than a mirror.
- Sleeping facing south.
- A sprig of white heather.
- A bluebird.
- A strange dog following you home.
- Putting your dress on inside out.
- Rubbing two horseshoes together.
- Picking up a pin.
- Catching two rats in the same trap.
- Sneezing three times before breakfast.
- Meeting a chimney sweep.

OMENS OF BAD LUCK

- An owl hooting three times (**a**).
- A five-leaved clover (**b**).
- Peacock feathers (**c**).
- A rooster crowing at night (**d**).
- Meeting a pig immediately after a wedding (**e**).
- Opening an umbrella indoors.
- Emptying ashes after dark.
- A bat entering the house.
- Putting a hat on a bed.
- Singing before breakfast.
- Giving away a wedding present.
- Borrowing, lending or burning a broom.
- Bringing eggs into the house after dark.
- Cutting your nails on Friday.
- Bringing white lilac or hawthorn blossom into the house.
- Putting shoes on a chair or table.
- Killing a seagull.
- Mending a garment while you are wearing it.
- Dropping an umbrella.
- Seeing an owl in daytime.
- Keeping your slippers on a shelf above head height.
- Putting an umbrella on a table.
- Blossom and fruit growing together on the same branch (except on orange trees).
- Meeting a grave digger.
- Buttoning a button into the wrong button hole.
- Putting your left shoe on before your right.
- Sitting on a table without keeping one foot on the ground.
- Killing a cricket.
- A picture falling.
- Breaking your glass when proposing a toast.
- Dropping a glove.

- Getting out of bed left foot first.
- Putting a pair of bellows on a table.
- A ring breaking on your finger.
- Three butterflies together.
- Red and white flowers in the same arrangement.
- Bringing Christmas greenery into the house before December 24.
- Leaving Christmas decorations up after Twelfth Night.
- Looking at the new moon over your left shoulder.
- Taking anything out of the house on New Year's Day.
- Removing your wedding ring.
- Meeting a hare on the road.
- Violets flowering out of season.
- Wearing an opal unless you were born in October.
- Putting your shirt on inside out.

ONEIROMANCY

Definition Using dreams to foretell the future.

History Divination by dreams is known all over the world. Although the exact origins of oneiromancy are not known, the oldest surviving comprehensive book of dreams and their meanings was compiled by Artemidorus of Ephesus in the second century. During the seventeenth century this work was translated into English, reprinted 32 times before 1800. It still influences dream dictionaries today. Another early example of dream lore was a papyrus of c.1250 B.C. which recorded around 200 dreams and their interpretations according to the god Horus. Aristotle argued that precognitive dreams were impossible. However, according to the Bible, the Pharaoh's precognitive dream of seven fat kine and seven lean kine (in the book of Genesis) was correctly interpreted by Joseph as prophesying seven fat years and seven lean years for Egypt. Perhaps one of the most famous precognitive dreams is that of Abraham Lincoln, who foresaw his own assassination.

Modern methods You can practice oneiromancy by following the instructions provided here and using a dream dictionary to help with your interpretation.

Equipment You do not need any equipment although some people like to keep a notebook and a pencil by their beds so that they can record their dreams as soon as they wake.

Identifying precognitive dreams

Precognitive dreams are thought to occur between 3:00 A.M. and 7:00 A.M. as this is the time when digestion has been completed and the mind and the body are both relaxed. The following dreams do not foretell the future and therefore have no prophetic value:

a Those concerning events of the previous day.
b Those with a reasonable outside cause, such as sleeping position, noise, temperature, etc.
c Those caused by indigestion or illness.
d Those occurring during the early part of the night.
e Those caused by a disturbing television program, book, film, etc.

Classifying dream images

In addition to using a dream dictionary for an
identification of symbol meanings, you should take into
account the overall classification of certain images as
shown below.

Type of dream/image	Meaning
Ascending in any way, e.g. up stairs, ladders, ropes, escalators.	Success. The higher you ascend, the greater the success.
Descending or falling in any way, e.g. down stairs, ladders, ropes, escalators.	Reverses or failures. The lower you descend, the greater the setbacks.
Clean, shiny objects	Omens of good fortune.
Dirty, dull objects	Omens of ill fortune.
Sharp objects, e.g. knife, sword, scissors, etc.	Bad news to come.
Being entertained	Can mean either good or ill fortune depending on whether you enjoyed or disliked being entertained.

Dreams of contrary

The meaning in some types of diagram is opposite that of the image. For example, misery and crying in a dream are thought to be omens of happiness.

Dreams of contrary include:

Criticism/appreciation	luxury/poverty
fear/courage	rejoycing/regrets
calm/disturbance	inferiority/superiority
ambition/setbacks	encouragement/
quarrels/affection	discouragement
losses/gains	

Obstacles in dreams

These represent the severity of difficulties facing you. For example, a small ditch that can be jumped suggests a minor obstacle, while a large ditch that cannot be easily crossed suggests a larger obstacle.

Obstacle dreams include:
abyss, barefoot, bolts, canyon, cave, cavern, cliffs, crutches, ditch, drawer, embankment, envelope, examinations, fence, floods, gate, gravel, hedge, hills, hunting, island, jumping, labyrinth, locks, mountain, prison, questions, rivalry, rocks, sewing, struggling, tower, traffic, valley, walking, wall, window, zipper.

Dreams with mixed meaning

In your interpretation you should bear in mind that many images foretell either good or ill fortune. For example, calm water indicates good fortune, rough water, difficulties.

Before you begin with your dream interpretation it is
important to identify any images within the dream that
might relate to aspects of your everyday life, or events
in your recent past or childhood. You should not
include these images in your interpretation as they are
not considered to be prophetic. Other images can be
used, however, and you should use the dream

Dream Dictionary

Dream image	Meaning
Abandoning	Being abandoned—troubles will end; abandoning another—trouble coming.
Abbey	Seen in daylight—good luck; seen at night—temporary sadness.
Abdomen	Pain in abdomen—good health; abdomen exposed—treachery.
Abroad	If you go—change, upheaval; if others go—enemies will be overcome.
Absence	Of a friend or love—emotional difficulties.
Accident	Be on your guard.
Accountant, accounts	Take greater care of your money.
Acid	Broken promises.
Acorn	Good fortune, happiness.
Acrobat	Beware of accidents, especially when traveling.
Acting	If you are acting—temporary troubles; if others are acting—travel.
Admiral	Successful social life.

dictionary to identify their meanings. The more clearly you remember a dream, the greater the significance is thought to be. Always begin your assessment with the image you recall most clearly, but remember to include all other details—however small—in your final, overall interpretation.

Dream image	Meaning
Adultery	If you commit it—betrayal by friend; if you resist it—happiness.
Adventure	Good fortune.
Advertisement	Placing an advertisement—avoid speculation; reading an advertisement—plans will work out.
Aerial, antenna	Extra money.
Age	Yourself in old age—illness; other old people—good luck.
Agony	Great joy.
Airplane	Good news, financial benefit.
Alarm	Exciting, profitable news.
Alcohol	In moderation—success; in excess—embarrassment.
Alien	New friends, major changes.
Alligator, crocodile	Beware enemies.
Almond, almond tree	Good fortune. Bitter almonds—a warning.
Alphabet	Good news coming.

continued

Dream Dictionary (continued)

Dream image	Meaning
Altar	Release from worry.
Ambulance	Important hopes fulfilled.
Amputation	Performed on you—a useful gain; performed on others—setbacks coming.
Ancestors	Unexpected honors.
Anchor	Economize.
Angel	Protection, success, happiness.
Anger	Achievement, useful assistance.
Animals	If calm—business success; if hostile—business reverses.
Ankles	Your own—success after a struggle; belonging to someone of the same sex—a problem solved; belonging to someone of the opposite sex—an unwise affair.
Antiques	Looking at antiques—happiness at home; buying them—an eventual inheritance; selling them—don't lend or borrow money.
Ants	Beneficial changes are coming. Infesting house—hard work and frustration ahead; on food—happiness.
Anvil	Great good fortune.
Ape	A mischief maker.
Apron	Financial improvement.
Arch	If whole—present efforts will be successful; if broken—change of direction needed.
Arm	Pleasant company.

Dream image	Meaning
Army	Obstacles ahead.
Arrow	Wounded by arrow—betrayal; broken arrow—a broken relationship.
Artist	Time is being wasted.
Ashes	Setbacks. From a cremation—an unexpected inheritance; emptying ashes—financial difficulties.
Atlas	Travel
Attic	Casual promiscuity.
Author	Widening interests, but don't lend money.
Avalanche	Seeing one—serious obstacles ahead; buried by one—good luck; others being buried—change of surroundings.
Award	Good fortune.
Baby	Attractive baby—good friends; ugly—treacherous friends; helpless—difficulties ahead; walking—sudden independence; several babies—satisfaction.
Back	If bare—loss of status; your own back—problems will disappear.
Badge	Security.
Bag	Paper—money troubles; cloth—financial improvement; leather—travel.
Baking	Improving fortunes.
Baldness	Your own—ill health; of others—betrayal.

continued

Dream Dictionary (continued)

Dream image	Meaning
Ball games	Good news, good friendship.
Balloon	Setbacks and misfortunes.
Bandage	New influences.
Banquet	Good fortune.
Barbecue	Imposed on by relatives.
Barber	Success after difficulties.
Bath	Empty—keep your temper; taking a bath—sorrow.
Battles	Serious quarrels.
Beans	Difficulties ahead. Cooking beans—increasing income.
Beard	A good omen, the fuller the better.
Bed	A strange bed—improved circumstances; your own bed—security; making a bed—unexpected visitors.
Beer	Success. Flat beer—failure.
Bees	Good news and financial success. Killing bees—ruin; beeswax—love affair; empty beehive—financial difficulties.
Beetles	Beware enemies. Killing beetles—temporary difficulties.
Beggar	Help coming.
Bell	One bell—bad news; several bells—good news; church bells—opposition; high belfry—good news.
Belt	Happy future.

Dream image	Meaning
Bench	Important business news.
Bereavement	Happiness.
Berries	Well-being and achievement.
Bicycle	Unexpected help.
Birds	Good fortune. Dead birds—bad times coming.
Birth	Achievement.
Bishop	Unpleasant news.
Black	Any black object is an ill omen.
Blemish	On neck, chest, or arms—success in love; on body or legs—scandal.
Blindness	Beware of deceit.
Blood	Your own—avoid hostility in the family; blood of others—beware of enemies.
Boat	A symbol for your life. The omen corresponds with what the boat is doing—smooth sailing, becalmed, etc.
Bones	Human—unexpected income; animal—financial setbacks; fish—illness; animal eating bones—ruin.
Books	Happiness and contentment.
Bottle	Full—prosperity; empty—loss; spilled—domestic quarrels; bottle of wine—bad temper; bottle of perfume—happiness; bottle of brandy—good news.
Bread	Fresh—good fortune; stale—family troubles; buying bread—success.

continued

Dream Dictionary (continued)

Dream image	Meaning
Breakfast	Misfortune.
Bricks	Sudden, unfavorable change.
Bride	Good fortune.
Bridegroom	Unexpected delays.
Bruise	Avoid high living.
Bubbles	Difficulties will be short lived. Blowing bubbles—beware of extravagance.
Burglar	Improved finances.
Burial	A birth or a wedding.
Burning	Increased prosperity.
Butterfly	Social success.
Button	New and shiny—good fortune; lost—beware overspending.
Cake	Happy times, achievement.
Calendar	Worries disappearing gradually.
Call	Your own name—important news; another's name—disruption ahead.
Camera	Deceit and troubles.
Camp	Good fortune.
Candle	Lit—good fortune; unlit—domestic disappointment; guttering—new opportunities; candlestick—social activity.
Cannon	Achievement.
Cap	End of troubles. Worn and dirty cap—minor reverses.
Carpentry	Enjoyment, security, love, leisure.

Dream image	Meaning
Carpet	Good luck.
Carrots	A legacy.
Castle	In good repair—good fortune; in ruins—curb your temper.
Cat	Treachery and deceit.
Catastrophe	Complete change of lifestyle.
Cattle	Peace and prosperity.
Cemetery	Good fortune.
Chains	Worries soon over.
Chair	Comfort, unexpected news. Rocking chair—legacy.
Cheese	Eating cheese—luck in love and money; strong-smelling cheese—embarrassment; processed cheese—need for change; grated cheese—money coming; making cheese—business success.
Children	Business success.
Chimney	Very high—unusual achievement; average size—favorable times ahead; smoking—good news; on fire—avoid antagonizing others; in bad repair—trouble; collapsed—a celebration.
Chips	Wood chips—irritations; gaming chips—successful speculation; potato chips—change for the better.
Church	Seen from outside—good fortune; seen from inside—trouble ahead.

continued

Dream Dictionary (continued)

Dream image	Meaning
Circus	Financial good fortune.
Cleaning	Beware being drawn into something illegal.
Clock	Don't waste time.
Clothing	Plenty of clothes—ill luck; lack of clothes—prosperity.
Coffee	Good news, happiness. If bitter—broken friendship; if spilled—small disappointments.
Coins	Unexpected income: the smaller the coin, the greater the gain. If counterfeit—minor illness.
Comet	Setbacks and opposition.
Committee	An upheaval.
Cooking	Good fortune, material well-being. If cooking soup—a rise to a position of power.
Corn	Great good fortune.
Cough	Danger from fire, flood or pestilence.
Court	Financial setbacks.
Crash	Important achievement.
Crime	If seen—beneficial changes; if you commit it—success on the way; if you are caught in the act—curb your tongue.
Crockery	Domestic happiness. Broken crockery—an unwanted change.
Cross	Adversity followed by good fortune.
Crowd	Happiness. Angry mob—danger.

Dream image	Meaning
Cuckoo	Upsetting news.
Curtains	Unknown enemies are about.
Cushions	Economies.
Dagger	Beware treachery.
Dam	Beware impulsive actions.
Dancing	New friends, social success.
Dawn	New opportunities, improved conditions.
Death	Your own—a change for the better; someone else's—a birth, unexpected good news.
Devil	Resist temptation, beware hidden enemies.
Directory	A good time for flirtation and gambling.
Dirt	Illness.
Dish	Full—good luck; empty—static period; broken—domestic difficulties.
Dizziness	Passionate attraction.
Doctor	Good fortune.
Dog	Good omen if friendly, the larger the better.
Doll	Domestic happiness.
Dragon	Assistance from a poweful person.
Drill	Stop wasting time.
Drowning	Business reverse.
Drugs	Warning against unwise decisions.

continued

Dream Dictionary (continued)

Dream image	Meaning
Drunkeness	Your own—beware of dissipation; someone else's—a loss.
Dust	Minor setbacks.
Ears	Surprising news. Painful ears—treachery; pierced ears—domestic loss; earrings—avoid gossip.
Earth	Profits.
Eggs	Contentment, prosperity.
Elastic	Your capabilities will be tested.
Election	Short-term success. Casting your vote—a wish coming true; ballot box—you need a change of lifestyle.
Elephant	Good fortune.
Eloping	A romantic disappointment.
Embarrassment	Success, well-being.
Embezzlement	Seek professional advice.
Enemies	Aid coming from loyal friends.
Engagement	Romantic troubles.
Escaping	Heading for success.
Evening	Increasing contentment in later life.
Evergreens	Success with money.
Execution	Your own—good health; someone else's—setbacks ahead.
Extravagance	Domestic happiness.
Eyes	Strange eyes—a beneficial change; painful eyes—beware deceit; attractive eyes—lucky in love; eyelids—someone

Dream image	Meaning
	else's troubles; false eyelashes—discovering secrets.
Faces	Pleasant—happiness, prosperity; unpleasant—loss, strangers' faces—a change of place; washing your face—troubles you have caused yourself.
Factory	Success after a struggle.
Fear	Difficulties will be overcome.
Feathers	Good luck, social popularity.
Feet	Large, bare feet—good luck; painful feet—trouble; itchy feet—travel.
Fever	An end to worries.
Fighting	Major changes, upheaval.
Fire	To see one—trouble; to make one—a new romance; to be burned—bad luck; a fireplace—contentment; a fire engine—money luck.
Fish	Catching them—prosperity; dead fish—disappointment; tropical fish—ephemeral pleasures.
Flag	Good times, financial improvement.
Flies	Petty annoyances.
Floating	Success, prosperity.
Floor	Profitable business activities.
Flowers	Bright and fresh—personal happiness; dead—beware of overconfidence; wild—an exciting adventure; artificial—don't act against your conscience.

continued

Dream Dictionary (continued)

Dream image	Meaning
Flying	Ambition achieved.
Food	Preparing fresh food—good fortune; lack of food—reverses; selling food—money luck; buying food—a celebration; tasting food—loss of property.
Footprints	Difficulties.
Footsteps	Learning something to your advantage.
Forest	Release from worries.
Fork	Decision to be made.
Fountain	Fulfillment.
Friends	Happy times, good news.
Fruit	Ripe—good luck; unripe, sour—bad luck.
Furniture	In good condition—good luck; in poor condition—bad luck.
Gallows	Good luck.
Gambling	Losing—financial success; winning—losses.
Gangway	A period of transition.
Garage	Improvements.
Garlic	Protection.
Ghost	Good fortune. Frightened by a ghost—beware ill-considered ventures.
Giant	Obstacles and enemies overcome.
Giggling	Financial embarrassment but social success.

Dream image	Meaning
Gloves	Your own—emotional security; new—financial security; lost—rely on your own resources; found—unexpected help; dirty—disappointments.
Goat	Avoid gambling and anything illegal.
Gold	Guard your possessions. Gold objects—financial luck.
Gondola	Romantic boredom.
Gong	Excitement.
Grain	Prosperity.
Grave	Loss and sadness.
Greenhouse	Love, success.
Gun	You will be wronged in some way.
Gypsy	Uncertainty, travel.
Hammer	Achievement, good luck.
Hand	Clean and well-kept—good fortune; injured—misfortune.
Handcuffs	Your worries are over.
Handkerchief	Quarrels, hostility.
Hangover	Family worries solved.
Harem	Busy social life, gossip.
Hay	Dry and sunlit—money troubles; wet or in a stack—money luck.
Hearse	Seeing a hearse—responsibilities lightening; riding in a hearse—responsibilities increasing.

continued

Dream Dictionary (continued)

Dream image	Meaning
Heat	Keep your temper.
Helmet	Problems caused by lack of organization.
Hiding	If you are hiding—beware ill-considered actions; if an object is hiding—take others' advice.
Hinge	Family difficulties, gossip.
Hole	Digging one—travel; being in one—false friends; holes in clothes—financial benefits.
Holiday	Hard work coming before any respite possible.
Honey	General good fortune.
Hood	Deception.
Horn	Good news; improved social life.
Horse	Good luck, success. Horse being shod—money; falling off a horse—misfortune.
Hospital	As a patient—do not overtax yourself; as a visitor—good news.
Hotel	Lucky in love.
House	Security and well-being. Derelict house—grief; buying a house—a love affair; selling a house—release from responsibilities; large house—wealth; small house—money troubles.
Hunger	Good times coming.
Ice	Success after adversity. Slipping on ice—difficulties ahead.

Dream image	Meaning
Iceberg	Hidden opposition.
Illness	Temptation, a dilemma.
Income	Large—financial failure; small—financial success.
Inheritance	A legacy or inheritance.
Injury	Recognition.
Ink	A problem solved.
Insects	Trivial difficulties.
Insult	A rise in status, loyalty, esteem.
Invalid	Delayed success.
Invisibility	Beneficial changes coming.
Invitations	Financial gains.
Island	New developments.
Itching	Stop worrying.
Ivy	Wealth and happiness.
Jail	Hardship ahead.
Jealousy	A series of problems, hostility.
Jewelry	Valuable jewelry—good fortune; costume jewelry—vanity; giving or receiving jewelry—lucky in love.
Job	Looking for a job or being fired—good luck.
Journey	Changes. Boat journey—friendship; airplane journey—quarrels.
Judge	Setbacks and hardships.
Jug	New and good friends.

continued

Dream Dictionary (continued)

Dream image	Meaning
Juggler	Easy profits.
Jungle	Avoid risky financial or emotional entanglements.
Kettle	Boiling—good luck; boiled dry—unexpected expenses.
Keys	In a lock—pleasurable love affair; finding, giving, or receiving keys—good luck; losing keys—bad luck; broken—lost opportunity; keyhole—treachery.
Killing	Human killed—avoid emotional upheaval; animal killed—help is on the way.
Kiss	Pleasure and contentment. Avoiding a kiss—a minor illness; kissing babies,success in a difficult task.
Knife	Ill fortune.
Knight	Protection.
Knitting	Peace of mind.
Knots	Anxiety.
Lamp	If lit—success; if you light it—benefit from past efforts; if you put it out—a rest or holiday.
Lateness	Trouble, deception.
Laughter	Ill luck in love and friendship.
Lava	Exciting social life.
Lawyer	Business worries.
Leaves	Green and growing—health and happiness; falling—a parting.
Light	Good fortune.

Dream image	Meaning
Lion	Social and financial advancement.
Lizard	Beware false friends.
Log	Good luck and happiness.
Love	Happiness and contentment.
Machinery	Running and well-tended—success; idle or derelict, employment problems.
Man	Family prosperity. Several men—nervous strain.
Map	Change, travel.
Mask	Deceit.
Meat	Business prosperity.
Mending	Unexpected windfall.
Messenger	A lucrative offer.
Milk	Fresh milk—good health; sour or spilled milk—illness.
Mirror	Dishonesty and disloyalty.
Money	Good fortune.
Moon	Waxing—a change for the better; waning—a change for the worse.
Mouth	Keep silent.
Music	Pleasant music—good fortune, happiness; discordant—ill fortune; playing an instrument—sudden changes.
Neck	Good luck financially. Broken neck—money mismanagement.

continued

Dream Dictionary (continued)

Dream image	Meaning
Needle	Bad luck. Threading a needle with ease—good luck.
Newspaper	Good fortune, happy times.
Night	Obstacles, delays.
Nose	Sore or injured—trouble, opposition; blowing your nose—the end of a bad time.
Nudity	Your own—financial and social success; of others—beware deceit.
Nurse	Family unity.
Nuts	Good fortune. Cracking nuts—health, success.
Office	Changes ahead in personal relationships.
Oil	Finances improving.
Operation	Major changes ahead.
Orchard	Achievement and satisfaction.
Orders	Obeying them—better times ahead; giving them—domestic discord.
Ornaments	Personal ornaments—improved prospects; household ornaments—setbacks; broken ornaments—good luck.
Oven	Cold—regrets; warm or hot—fruitful efforts.
Owl	Setbacks and disappointments.
Painting	A house—beware ill-considered actions; a picture—circumstances improving.

Dream image	Meaning
Paper	Effort and opportunity.
Paralysis	Internal conflict.
Parents	Happiness and achievement. Becoming a parent—unexpected news.
Park	A new and happy love affair.
Party	Social pleasure.
Pearls	Prosperity through hard work.
Pebbles	Gossip, depression.
Pendulum	Unexpected changes.
Perfume	Used by a woman—a new love affair; used by a man—misunderstanding.
Photographs	Happy friendships.
Pictures	Treachery.
Pigs	Troubles at home but progress at work.
Pins	Finding one—good luck; being pricked by one—trouble; in use on clothing— trouble; full pincusion—achievement.
Politics	Success, responsibilities.
Power	The greater the power, the greater your achievement.
Prize	Success and achievement.
Publicity	Be diplomatic.
Puppets	Fear of being manipulated.
Pyramid	Success, enjoyable change, and travel.
Quarrel	Peace and happiness in personal relationships.

continued

Dream Dictionary (continued)

Dream image	Meaning
Quilt	Prosperity, domestic bliss.
Rabbits	Satisfying changes, prosperity.
Race	Success, advancement.
Raft	Enforced travel.
Rain	Good fortune and prosperity, unless you are already wealthy in which case it means bad luck.
Rainbow	Troubles ending.
Rats	Ill fortune, hidden enemies.
Razor	Control yourself.
Refrigerator	Propserity, unexpected guests.
Relatives	Freedom from worry, help when needed.
Restaurant	Cheap—improved finances; modest—social happiness; expensive—setbacks.
Ring	Financial and romantic success.
Roof	In good repair—good luck; repairing one—finances improving; leaky roof—unhappiness in love; roof on fire—stop worrying; falling off roof—temporary success.
Rope	Success, beneficial changes.
Ruins	Improving conditions.
Running	Toward something—fulfillment; away from something—trouble, hardship; unable to run—lack of self-confidence.
Sacrifice	Rejoicing.
Salt	Great good fortune.

Dream image	Meaning
Sand	Beware of new acquaintances.
Scandal	Examine your conscience.
Scarf	Happiness in love.
School	Seeing a school—financial gain; being at school—difficulties; leaving school—temporary financial gain.
Screaming	Hearing a scream—bad news; screaming yourself—good luck.
Secrets	Beware deceit and malice.
Sex	Enjoyable and satisfying—good fortune; being a different sex—a change for the better.
Shadow	Your own—improved finances; someone else's—dangers ahead.
Shells	Unusual events.
Signature	Good luck, security.
Silver	Coins—improved finances; objects—beware too much concern with money.
Snake	Ill luck.
Snow	Happiness and prosperity after temporary setbacks.
Spider	Good luck, success.
Spies	Impulsive behavior.
Spoons	Domestic bliss. Lost or stolen—unwise investments.
Stains	Scandals, laziness.
Star	Fulfillment, happiness.

continued

Dream Dictionary (continued)

Dream image	Meaning
Storms	Discontentment.
Strangers	Happy reunion.
Sun	Success, happiness. Sunrise or sunset—beneficial changes.
Swamps	Threats to finances and emotional life.
Swimming	Good fortune.
Table	Improving fortunes. Kitchen table—hard work ahead.
Tea	Social success.
Teeth	Aching or damaged teeth—ill luck; teeth in good condition, or false teeth—good luck.
Telephone	Rivalry, sad news.
Thorns	Malicious associates.
Thunder	Loud—good luck; distant, rumbling—treachery.
Towel	Clean—health, material prosperity; wet—frustration; paper—recession.
Toys	Whole—good luck; broken—stop behaving childishly.
Trial	Be cautious.
Tunnel	Changes bringing risks.
Umbrella	Achievement, security. Broken—reverses; inside out—achievement after hardship.
Undressing	Misplaced confidence and affections.
Uniform	Security, happiness, and advancement.
Vampire	Anxiety.

Dream image	Meaning
Vegetables	Growing or cooking them—good times coming; eating them—troubles ahead; rotten vegetables—ill luck.
Visitor	Being a visitor—beware false friends; being visited—beware actions that will harm others.
Volcano	Disagreements, dishonesty.
Walking	Obstacles will disappear.
Washing	Yourself—new friends; objects—upheavals.
Watch	Advancement through positive action.
Wheels	Progress. The speed of progress increases with the speed at which the wheels turn.
Whispering	Think before you speak or act.
Whistling	Setbacks, difficulties, criticism.
Wine	Health, happiness.
Woman	Increasing prosperity and security.
Worms	Alive—illness; killing worms or using them as bait—good fortune.
Writing	Your writing—beware making trouble for yourself; someone else's writing—beware bad advice.
X-rays	Good health.
Yawn	Setbacks of your own making.
Zoo	Unexpected but enjoyable travel.

ORIENTAL ASTROLOGY

Definition A form of Eastern divination based on a 12-year cycle and involving 12 animals, the characteristics of which are thought to influence individual personality and to govern the nature of years themselves. Unlike the signs of the zodiac used in Western astrology (e.g. Aries, Taurus, Gemini), the animals unique to Oriental astrology do not rely on the configuration or movements of planets.

History Legend has it that Buddha invited all the animals to celebrate the New Year with him but only 12 came—the rat, ox, tiger, rabbit, dragon, snake, horse, goat, monkey, rooster, dog, and pig. As a reward for their attendance, Buddha named a year after each animal, according to the order in which they arrived in his presence. Oriental astrology is therefore based on a 12-year cycle. The ancient Chinese consulted a horoscope disk known as the lo-king, using it to predict the future. On the lo-king, the stars and planets are in the center with the 12 animal signs around the outside. In Vietnam, the year of the rabbit is known as the year of the cat. Every 60 years is a special year for the horse and is known as the year of the fire horse.

Modern methods Oriental astrology has remained the same for many hundreds of years. In the same way that many people in the West known their sun sign, many people in the East know the animal that rules their date of birth. Each of the 12 animal years in the Oriental 12-year cycle is a lunar year, and therefore begins on a different date according to the Western calendar—any time between January 21 and February 21.

Equipment To find out your animal sign, you need to know your date of birth. Consult the table of years provided here to find which animal governs the year of your birth. Once you have identified your sign, turn to the information presented about that sign in order to discover what are supposed to be your good and bad points, and the signs with which you are most compatible. Also consult the table showing the influence of years to see which years are good for you, which bad, and which indifferent.

Oriental astrology is complex and it is impossible to give a full description here. More detailed information about all 12 animal signs can be found in *The Little Giant Encyclopedia of the Zodiac*.

TABLE OF YEARS

Jan 31, 1900 – Feb 17, 1912			
1900	Jan 31, 1900	–	Feb 18, 1901	Rat
1901	Feb 19, 1901	–	Feb 7, 1902	Ox
1902	Feb 8, 1902	–	Jan 28, 1903	Tiger
1903	Jan 29, 1903	–	Feb 15, 1904	Rabbit
1904	Feb 16, 1904	–	Feb 3, 1905	Dragon
1905	Feb 4, 1905	–	Jan 24, 1906	Snake
1906	Jan 25, 1906	–	Feb 12, 1907	Horse
1907	Feb 13, 1907	–	Feb 1, 1908	Goat
1908	Feb 2, 1908	–	Jan 21, 1909	Monkey
1909	Jan 22, 1909	–	Feb 9, 1910	Rooster
1910	Feb 10, 1910	–	Jan 29, 1911	Dog
1911	Jan 30, 1911	–	Feb 17, 1912	Pig

Feb 18, 1912 – Feb 4, 1924

1912	Feb 18, 1912 – Feb 5, 1913	Rat
1913	Feb 6, 1913 – Jan 25, 1914	Ox
1914	Jan 26, 1914 – Feb 13, 1915	Tiger
1915	Feb 14, 1915 – Feb 2, 1916	Rabbit
1916	Feb 3, 1916 – Jan 22, 1917	Dragon
1917	Jan 23, 1917 – Feb 10, 1918	Snake
1918	Feb 11, 1918 – Jan 31, 1919	Horse
1919	Feb 1, 1919 – Feb 19, 1920	Goat
1920	Feb 20, 1920 – Feb 7, 1921	Monkey
1921	Feb 8, 1921 – Jan 27, 1922	Rooster
1922	Jan 28, 1922 – Feb 15, 1923	Dog
1923	Feb 16, 1923 – Feb 4, 1924	Pig

Feb 5, 1924 – Jan 23, 1936

1924	Feb 5, 1924 – Jan 24, 1925	Rat
1925	Jan 25, 1925 – Feb 12, 1926	Ox
1926	Feb 13, 1926 – Feb 1, 1927	Tiger
1927	Feb 2, 1927 – Jan 22, 1928	Rabbit
1928	Jan 23, 1928 – Feb 9, 1929	Dragon
1929	Feb 10, 1929 – Jan 29, 1930	Snake
1930	Jan 30, 1930 – Feb 16, 1931	Horse
1931	Feb 17, 1931 – Feb 5, 1932	Goat
1932	Feb 6, 1932 – Jan 25, 1933	Monkey
1933	Jan 26, 1933 – Feb 13, 1934	Rooster
1934	Feb 14, 1934 – Feb 3, 1935	Dog
1935	Feb 4, 1935 – Jan 23, 1936	Pig

Jan 24, 1936 – Feb 9, 1948

1936	Jan 24, 1936 – Feb 10, 1937	Rat
1937	Feb 11, 1937 – Jan 30, 1938	Ox
1938	Jan 31, 1938 – Feb 18, 1939	Tiger
1939	Feb 19, 1939 – Feb 7, 1940	Rabbit
1940	Feb 8, 1940 – Jan 26, 1941	Dragon
1941	Jan 27, 1941 – Feb 14, 1942	Snake
1942	Feb 15, 1942 – Feb 4, 1943	Horse
1943	Feb 5, 1943 – Jan 24, 1944	Goat
1944	Jan 25, 1944 – Feb 12, 1945	Monkey
1945	Feb 13, 1945 – Feb 1, 1946	Rooster
1946	Feb 2, 1946 – Jan 21, 1947	Dog
1947	Jan 22, 1947 – Feb 9, 1948	Pig

Feb 10, 1948 – Jan 27, 1960

1948	Feb 10, 1948 – Jan 28, 1949	Rat
1949	Jan 29, 1949 – Feb 16, 1950	Ox
1950	Feb 17, 1950 – Feb 5, 1951	Tiger
1951	Feb 6, 1951 – Jan 26, 1952	Rabbit
1952	Jan 27, 1952 – Feb 13, 1953	Dragon
1953	Feb 14, 1953 – Feb 2, 1954	Snake
1954	Feb 3, 1954 – Jan 23, 1955	Horse
1955	Jan 24, 1955 – Feb 11, 1956	Goat
1956	Feb 12, 1956 – Jan 30, 1957	Monkey
1957	Jan 31, 1957 – Feb 17, 1958	Rooster
1958	Feb 18, 1958 – Feb 7, 1959	Dog
1959	Feb 8, 1959 – Jan 27, 1960	Pig

Jan 28, 1960 – Feb 14, 1972

1960	Jan 28, 1960 – Feb 14, 1961	Rat
1961	Feb 15, 1961 – Feb 4, 1962	Ox
1962	Feb 5, 1962 – Jan 24, 1963	Tiger
1963	Jan 25, 1963 – Feb 12, 1964	Rabbit
1964	Feb 13, 1964 – Feb 1, 1965	Dragon
1965	Feb 2, 1965 – Jan 20, 1966	Snake
1966	Jan 21, 1966 – Feb 8, 1967	Horse
1967	Feb 9, 1967 – Jan 29, 1968	Goat
1968	Jan 30, 1968 – Feb 16, 1969	Monkey
1969	Feb 17, 1969 – Feb 5, 1970	Rooster
1970	Feb 6, 1970 – Jan 26, 1971	Dog
1971	Jan 27, 1971 – Feb 14, 1972	Pig

Feb 15, 1972 – Feb 1, 1984

1972	Feb 15, 1972 – Feb 2, 1973	Rat
1973	Feb 3, 1973 – Jan 22, 1974	Ox
1974	Jan 23, 1974 – Feb 10, 1975	Tiger
1975	Feb 11, 1975 – Jan 30, 1976	Rabbit
1976	Jan 31, 1976 – Feb 17, 1977	Dragon
1977	Feb 18, 1977 – Feb 6, 1978	Snake
1978	Feb 7, 1978 – Jan 27, 1979	Horse
1979	Jan 28, 1979 – Feb 15, 1980	Goat
1980	Feb 16, 1980 – Feb 4, 1981	Monkey
1981	Feb 5, 1981 – Jan 24, 1982	Rooster
1982	Jan 25, 1982 – Feb 12, 1983	Dog
1983	Feb 13, 1983 – Feb 1, 1984	Pig

Feb 2, 1984 – Feb 18, 1996

1984	Feb 2, 1984 – Feb 19, 1985	Rat
1985	Feb 20, 1985 – Feb 8, 1986	Ox
1986	Feb 9, 1986 – Jan 28, 1987	Tiger
1987	Jan 29, 1987 – Feb 16, 1988	Rabbit
1988	Feb 17, 1988 – Feb 5, 1989	Dragon
1989	Feb 6, 1989 – Jan 26, 1990	Snake
1990	Jan 27, 1990 – Feb 14, 1991	Horse
1991	Feb 15, 1991 – Feb 3, 1992	Goat
1992	Feb 4, 1992 – Jan 22, 1993	Monkey
1993	Jan 23, 1993 – Feb 9, 1994	Rooster
1994	Feb 10, 1994 – Jan 30, 1995	Dog
1995	Jan 31, 1995 – Feb 18, 1996	Pig

Feb 19, 1996 – Feb 6, 2008

1996	Feb 19, 1996 – Feb 7, 1997	Rat
1997	Feb 8, 1997 – Jan 27, 1998	Ox
1998	Jan 28, 1998 – Feb 5, 1999	Tiger
1999	Feb 6, 1999 – Feb 4, 2000	Rabbit
2000	Feb 5, 2000 – Jan 23, 2001	Dragon
2001	Jan 24, 2001 – Feb 11, 2002	Snake
2002	Feb 12, 2002 – Jan 31, 2003	Horse
2003	Feb 1, 2003 – Jan 21, 2004	Goat
2004	Jan 22, 2004 – Feb 8, 2005	Monkey
2005	Feb 9, 2005 – Jan 28, 2006	Rooster
2006	Jan 29, 2006 – Feb 17, 2007	Dog
2007	Feb 18, 2007 – Feb 6, 2008	Pig

INFLUENCE OF THE YEARS

Year	What to do
Rat	• Expect political surprises • Save up for the future • Read good books that will be published
Ox	• Take care not to be overworked • Look after your garden • Enjoy the good harvest
Tiger	• Expect major changes in your life • Expect political upheavals • Try to find a little peace and quiet
Rabbit	• A year that allows you rest. Take advantage of this by taking holidays and enjoying the company of friends

Good for	Bad for	Indifferent for
Rat	Tiger	Snake
Ox	Rabbit	Dogs
Dragon	Horse	
Monkey	Goat	
Pig	Rooster	
Ox	Tiger	Rat
Horse	Snake	Rabbit
Monkey	Goat	Dragon
Rooster	Dogs	Pig
Tiger	Buffalo	Rabbit
Dragon	Rat	Snake
Horse	Rooster	Pig
Dog	Goat	Monkey
Rabbit	Rat	Ox
Dragon		Tiger
Snake		Rooster
Horse		Dog
Goat		Pig
Monkey		

INFLUENCE OF THE YEARS

Year	What to do
Dragon	• Enjoy a successful, exciting and exhausting year • Be enterprising and ambitious
Snake	• All your problems will appear to have been solved • Enjoy a lazy, hedonistic year
Horse	• There is irritability here. Get involved, but exercise tact with those around you who may have ruffled tempers
Goat	• Both you and the world muddle through a series of crises • Be yourself • Try to find time for a little self-indulgence

Good for	Bad for	Indifferent for
Rat	Dog	Ox
Tiger		Rabbit
Dragon		Snake
Monkey		Pig
Rooster		Horse
		Goat
Rabbit	Rat	Rooster
Dragon	Ox	Horse
Snake	Tiger	Pig
Goat		
Monkey		
Dog		
Ox	Horse	Tiger
Dragon	Rat	Rabbit
Goat	Snake	Monkey
Rooster	Pig	Dog
Goat	Ox	Rat
Monkey	Tiger	Rabbit
Pig	Rooster	Dragon
	Dog	Snake
		Horse

INFLUENCE OF THE YEARS

Year	What to do
Monkey	• A year in which you do not think before you act • Expect the unexpected • Launch some new ideas • Take some risks
Rooster	• The forces of law and order are in full cry • Unemployment rises • Watch your behavior • Keep scratching around to make a living
Dog	• There is a great deal of idealism and generosity around • You may feel defensive • Don't be too pessimistic
Pig	• An especially good year for anyone setting out to make money, and for intellectuals • There is enough of everything for everyone • Enjoy yourself

Good for	Bad for	Indifferent for
Rat	Ox	Rabbit
Tiger		Dragon
Horse		Snake
Goat		
Dog		
Pig		
Monkey		
Rooster		
Rat	Tiger	Ox
Dragon	Rabbit	Goat
Horse	Snake	Dog
Rooster		Monkey
Pig		
Rat	Ox	Tiger
Dragon	Snake	Rabbit
Dog	Goat	Horse
Pig	Rooster	Monkey
Rat	—	Ox
Tiger		Snake
Rabbit		Goat
Dragon		Rooster
Horse		Dog
Monkey		
Pig		

THE TWELVE ANIMAL SIGNS

Sign and character	Positive traits

THE RAT
- An opportunist
- A bargain hunter
- Hoards for the future
- Is frightened of failure
- Sentimental

- Charming
- Clever
- Elegant
- Light-hearted
- Can be a constructive critic

THE OX
- Down-to-earth
- Authoritarian in appearance
- A methodical mind hiding behind a conservative exterior

- Placid
- Patient
- Affectionate
- Clever
- Original

THE TIGER
- Respected leader
- Intensely emotional
- Sensitive
- Capable of grand, generous gestures as well as petty meanness
- Rebellious

- Magnetic
- Passionate
- Protective

Negative traits	Compatible with	Incompatible with
• Aggressive • A grumbler	Dragon Ox Monkey	Rabbit Horse
• Possessive • Can be introspective • Idealistic	Rooster Rat Snake	Monkey Goat Tiger
• Stubborn • Rash • A hothead • Lacks trust • Critical • Quarrelsome • Can be indecisive	Horse Dragon Dog	Snake Monkey Ox Rabbit

THE TWELVE ANIMAL SIGNS

Sign and character	Positive traits

THE RABBIT
- A friend who is a bit of a show off
- Peace-loving
- Enjoys company
- Sentimental
- Apparently mysterious
- Contented
- Proud and cautious

- Warm and affectionate
- Clever
- Sympathetic
- Industrious
- Entertains with traditional and generous hospitality

THE DRAGON
- A gifted, tenacious perfectionist who does everything thoroughly
- Proud
- Always succesful
- Loves show and spectacle
- Air of superiority hides deep discontent

- Generous
- Honest
- Enthusiastic
- Healthy
- Energetic

THE SNAKE
- A self-critical philosopher
- A good-natured snob
- Sentimental
- Romantic flirt
- Determined
- Slow to anger
- Helps in kind rather than cash

- Elegant
- Attractive
- Amusing
- Decisive
- Wise
- Intuitive
- Lucky with money

Negative traits	Compatible with	Incompatible with
• Condescending • Sometimes superficial	Goat Dog Pig	Rat Tiger Rooster
• Tactless • Idealistic	Rat Snake Rooster Monkey	Dog Ox
• Lazy • Cautious • Bad loser when crossed • Possessive • Tendency to exaggeration and ostentation	Rooster Ox Dragon Dog	Tiger Pig

THE TWELVE ANIMAL SIGNS

Sign and character	Positive traits

THE HORSE
- A popular extrovert
- Can succeed in most things when at center of attention
- Cunning
- Loves crowds and flattery
- A born politician
- Would give up all for love

- Quick-witted.
- Attractive
- Healthy

THE GOAT
- Happiest when supported by others who will bear all responsibility
- Craves security
- Is often the helpless center of attention
- Lacks a sense of time

- Graceful
- Creative

THE MONKEY
- An exuberant opportunist
- Curious
- Independent
- Ambitious
- Successful
- Prefers infatuation to love

- Intelligent
- Amusing
- Inventive
- Good memory
- Good with money

Negative traits	Compatible with	Incompatible with
• Impatient • Intemperate • Egotistical • Lacks self-confidence • Ignores advice	Goat Dog Tiger Rooster	Rat Monkey Ox Pig
• Weak-willed • A worrier • Lacks self-control • Has no respect for the property of others • Frequently discontented	Horse Pig Rabbit Monkey	Ox Dog
• Egotistical • Apparently friendly but really contemptuous • Vain • Unscrupulous • Easily bored	Dragon Rat Goat	Tiger Horse Pig

THE TWELVE ANIMAL SIGNS

Sign and character	Positive traits
THE ROOSTER • A popular daydreamer who likes people • Needs occasional solitude • Dislikes routine • Works well under pressure • Loves and needs to be praised	• Often succeeds beyond all expectations • Gives advice frankly
THE DOG • A shy idealist with a strong sense of justice • A hard worker • Antisocial • Intelligent • Not good with money	• Loyal • Honest • Reliable • Generous • Courageous • A good listener
THE PIG • Innocent • A pacifist • Occasionally becoming rich • Sensitive • Sensualist • An intellectual who reads indiscriminately	• Honest • Trusting • Gallant • A loyal friend • Courteous

Negative traits	Compatible with	Incompatible with
• Extravagant • A boaster • Often undertakes too much	Ox Snake Horse Dragon Dog Rat	Rabbit Other roosters
• Stubborn • An introverted worrier • Cynical • Pessimistic	Horse Tiger Rabbit	Dragon Goat
• Is easily taken advantage of • Stubborn • Scrupulous • Uncompromising • Sad	Rabbit Dragon	Goat Snake

PALMISTRY

Definition Method of predicting the future by "reading" the marks on a person's palm, but which also includes an analysis of hand shape, fingers and fingernails. Experts prefer terms such as "chirognomy," "chirology," or "chiromancy," from the Greek word *cheir*, meaning hand.

History Palmistry has had a checkered history: in the seventeenth century it was taught at the universities of Leipzig and Halle in Germany, while at the same time it was being outlawed in England as a form of witchcraft. Palm prints have been discovered in Stone Age cave paintings and although no physical evidence exists to support their theories, some practitioners have claimed that the origins of palmistry originate with the ancient Egyptians, Chaldeans, Sumerians, or Babylonians. It seems likely that palmistry began in the East and spread to the West, perhaps carried by the Romany peoples. Indian literature of the Vedic period (c. 2000 B.C.) in the East, and in the works of Aristotle (384-322 B.C.) in the West appear to be the earliest verifiable references to this method of prediction.

Modern methods The techniques used in palm reading have remained unchanged for centuries, although modern practitioners prefer to use four basic hand "classifications," believing that the seven traditional hand classifications are too rigid.

Equipment You do not need any special equipment for palmistry other than a palm to read. Alternatively, you can make a handprint and read from that.

General guidelines

Examine both hands Comparing the differences
between left and right hands can be useful for revealing
the directions the subject has taken through life, and the
effect of the years on the subject. Your left hand is said
to indicate the potentialities that you were born with,
and your right hand to reveal your individual nature as
it is now, and what the future may be—unless you are
left-handed, when the reverse applies.

Take an overall view It is not possible to ascertain the
exact nature of your subject's character and potential
from any isolated detail. It is essential to wait until you
have gathered all your clues and can then see how one
factor balances or compensates for another, how
different elements are reinforced, others cancelled out,
and so on.

Avoid sweeping statements Information gathered from
a person's hands cannot be interpreted simply, in the
way of the omens of folk belief, or the flat assertions of
newspaper horoscopes. Because there are many factors
to be taken into account in a subject as broad and
complex as palmistry, good palmists rarely make
sweeping, unequivocal statements such as, "you will be
rich this time next year" or "you have only six months
to live." Instead they prefer to generalize, since what
they achieve, when all the details are collated, is only a
probable pattern, a set of tendencies, with very little in
it of fixed, unavoidable fate. Every reading, like every
human being, is a mixture of good and bad.

Be careful You will need to have studied a great many
hands before you can be completely confident in your
recognition of detail—hands seldom show marks as

clearly as do the illustrations in this book.

Be open-minded Let your palm-reading skills build
slowly, and accept all the contradictions, divergences,
and inconsistencies. Don't leap to conclusions about the
nature of a hand, for there is then the temptation to
ignore other details, or subconsciously to twist their
meaning, when they do not conform to your too-hasty
interpretation.

Correlate all details Most people get through life with
plenty of ups and downs, facing good times and bad.
Bearing this in mind, try to obtain a complete, balanced
picture before delivering your interpretation.

Remember that destiny is not fixed The lines and
marks of a hand can change, it is said, over a period of
time, as can the fleshiness of the fingers and mounts.
And so good or ill omens may in fact come and go.
Chirognomists assert that destiny as revealed in the
hand is not fixed and predetermined.

Handprints

Using handprints for your readings means that you will
not be affected by your subject's reactions to your
comments. Also, if you keep the prints, they are useful
for comparison in years to come. Because aspects other
than the palm are important to palm reading (the size
and color of fingernails, for example) it is important
that you take a good look at your subject's hand when
making a print as a fully comprehensive reading cannot
be made from a print alone. For making handprints you
need some water-based ink (for easy removal), a roller
and some paper.

Making a handprint
1 Squeeze some ink onto a smooth surface and coat the roller with it.
2 Use the roller to transfer a thin film of ink as evenly as possible over your subject's palm.
3 Make the print by pressing your subject's hand carefully onto the paper.
4 Lift the hand away, making sure not to blur the print.

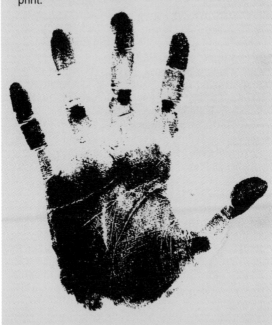

HAND CLASSIFICATIONS

There are two types of hand classification—the traditional and modern. Traditionally, fortune-tellers categorized seven basic types of hand shape. Modern palmists recognize four basic types but retain a traditional flavor by relating them to the four elements of the ancient world—earth, fire, water, and air—which are linked in turn to corresponding character traits. It does not really matter which classification you use, as either serves as a starting point for your reading, to which you will add information gathered from your examination of the palm, fingers, and fingernails.

Size and texture of hands The size and texture of people's hands can provide useful information as to their character. Proportionately large hands indicate a thoughtful, patient mind and a skill with fine, delicate, detailed work. People whose hands are small in comparison to the rest of their build will think and act on a large scale. Optimistic, healthy individuals often have a palm that is firm and elastic in texture; sensuality and indolence are indicated by a soft, flabby, and fleshy palm; a hard, dry, wooden palm indicates a tense, chronic worrier.

Traditional hand classifications

Traditional hand classifications reveal traditional attitudes to society and its hierarchy—at one end of the scale is the peasant's coarsened and work-hardened fist, and at the other is the delicate and languid hand of the aristocrat. Examples are shown here next to a standard hand shape.

Elemental

A thick, broad, short-fingered hand. A slow thinker, perhaps with a crude, physical nature.

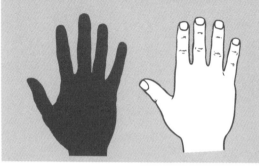

Square (or useful)

A square palm, with broad and blunt fingers. A practical, conventional, unadaptable, unintellectual nature.

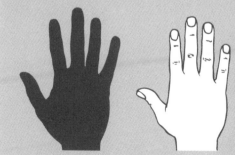

Philosophical
Broad-palmed, with heavy joints on the fingers. A logical, cautious nature, thoughtful and introverted, analytic rather than fanciful.

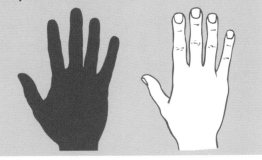

Mixed
A necessary, if vague, category. Almost no one fits precisely into just one pigeonhole. Most hands combine two or more of the types mentioned, as do most people's natures.

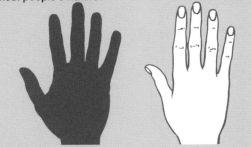

Artistic (or conic)
A long and flexible hand with tapering fingers. A sensitive, creative nature, more impulsive than methodical.

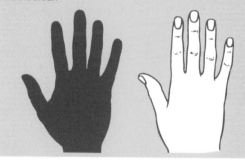

Idealistic
An even longer and more delicate hand. A nature far removed from harsh reality, a dreamer, mystic, aesthete.

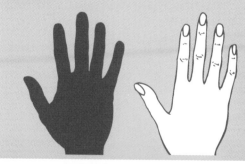

Spatulate
A spade-shaped and straight-fingered hand. An
ambitious and energetic nature, independent,
erratic, not much given to intellect.

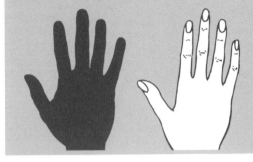

Modern hand classifications
Compare these modern hand classifications (illustrated
opposite) with earlier, traditional classifications.

Practical (a) square palm with short fingers. An honest,
hard-working, feet-on-the-ground person. Linked with
the element of earth.

Intuitive (b) A long palm with short fingers. An
energetic, restless, individualistic nature. Linked with
the element of fire.

Sensitive (c) A long palm with long fingers. An
imaginative, emotional nature, often moody or
introverted. Linked with the element of water.

Intellectual (d) A square palm with long fingers. A
clever, rational, articulate nature, aware and orderly
(sometimes too orderly). Linked with the element of air.

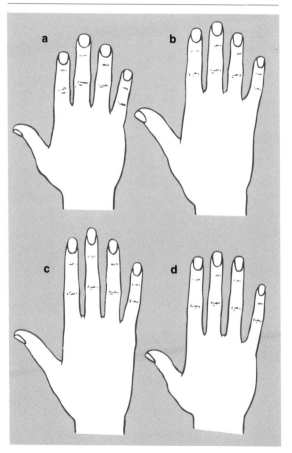

FINGERNAILS

Fingernails give important indications of a person's
state of health, which is why doctors may examine a
patient's fingertips when making an examination. The
shape and color of nails can provide clues to the
character of their owner. For example, we expect
people who bite their fingernails to be tense and
anxious.

Nail shapes

Shape	Character indication
Short nails (**a**)	Energetic, curious, intuitive, logical
Short nails, broader (**b**) than they are long	Critical and quick tempered
Broad, long nails, rounded at the tip (**c**)	A person of clear, sound judgement
Long, almond-shaped nails (**d**)	Placid and easy-going, a dreamer
Very large, square nails (**e**)	Cold and selfish
Wedge-shaped nails (**f**)	Oversensitive

a   b   c   d   e   f

Nail color

Color	Character indication
White	Cold, conceited, and selfish
Pale pink	A warm, and outgoing nature
Red	A violent temper
Bluish	Unhealthy

AREAS OF THE HAND

Each area of the hand
is thought to relate to a
particular facet of the
personality, and palmists
divide the hand
accordingly.

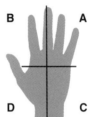

Area of hand	Relating to
A The inner active area	●Close relationships ●Sexuality
B The outer active area	●Social attitudes ●Relationships with the outside world
C The inner passive area	●The subconscious
D The outer passive area	●Energy ●Creative potential

FINGERS
Names and traits

In palmistry, fingers are named according to Roman gods (that are in most cases the names of planets), and each relates to a different aspect of character.

Finger	Name	Aspect of character
Index (**a**)	Jupiter	Outer, worldly tendencies—ambition, prospects for success, life energy
Middle (**b**)	Saturn	The saturnine qualities of character—seriousness and melancholy
Third or ring (**c**)	Apollo (the sun)	Inner concerns
Little (**d**)	Mercury	Human relationships

The set of the fingers

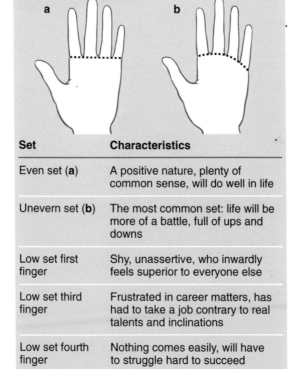

Set	Characteristics
Even set (**a**)	A positive nature, plenty of common sense, will do well in life
Unevern set (**b**)	The most common set: life will be more of a battle, full of ups and downs
Low set first finger	Shy, unassertive, who inwardly feels superior to everyone else
Low set third finger	Frustrated in career matters, has had to take a job contrary to real talents and inclinations
Low set fourth finger	Nothing comes easily, will have to struggle hard to succeed

Note: The second finger is never set low, but decides the level for the other fingers.

Hand span

Span type	Characteristics
Fingers held stiffly together	Cautious, suspicious, and unsociable
Unevenly spaced fingers	A well-balanced mind, likely to be successful in any field
Well-separated fingers	Independent and freedom loving
Wide gap between all fingers	Frank, open, and trusting—an almost child-like nature
Widest space between thumb and first finger	Outgoing, a generous disposition
Widest space between first and second fingers	Not easily influenced by others, independent in thought and action
Widest space between second and third fingers	Free from anxieties for the future, light-hearted
Widest space between third and fourth fingers	An independent and original thinker
Fourth finger very separated from the other fingers	Difficulties in personal relationships, isolated and alienated

Finger shapes

Shape	Characteristics
Long	Intelligent
Short	Impulsive, hasty
Large	Painstaking, slow-thinking
Smooth joints (**a**)	Quick-thinking, impulsive
Square (**b**)	Thoughtful, cautious
Spatulate (**c**)	Energetic
Waisted	Considerate
Slender	Introverted, aesthetic nature
Knotty joints (**d**)	Deep-thinking, dignified
Thick and short	Selfish
Crooked	Malicious, easily irritated
Tapered (**e**)	Impulsive, artistic, punctilious
Puffy	Hedonistic
Large joints	Methodical, rational

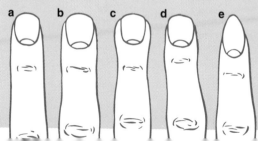

When making observations based on finger shapes, you should always take an overall view. For example, in a pointed, smooth-jointed finger we have a double indication of impulsiveness, whereas with a square, smooth-jointed finger, the reflective qualities of the square shape will balance the impulsive nature shown by the smooth joints.

Flexibility and bend of the fingers

Finger Characteristics	Suggested character traits
Stiff fingers	Stiff, unyielding, rigid, set in their ways, but also practically inclined
Curved fingers, bending toward the palm	Prudent and acquisitive nature
Curved and stiff fingers	Fearful, cautious, narrow-minded, tenacious
Supple fingers	Attractive, unconventional, somewhat careless
Curved fingers, bending away from palm	Ignores rules and regulations, chatty, good company
Backward curving and supple fingers	Open minded, inquisitive, attractive

THE FIRST, INDEX, OR FOREFINGER (Jupiter)

Characteristics	Suggested character
Top level with bottom of nail on second finger	A leader, a person with the power to govern
Top below bottom of nail on second finger	Timid, feels inferior, avoids responsibility
Same length as, or longer than, second finger	A dictator, self-centered, one determined to make others obey
Normal length, but shorter than third finger	A good organizer, capable of taking charge, but preferring to work in partnership
Top phalange bending toward second finger	Persistent, stubborn
Same length as third finger	Well-balanced and self-assured
Longer than third finger	Proud, ambitious, longing for power
Long and smooth	Good prospects in work, business and in the outside world in general

continued

THE FIRST, INDEX, OR FOREFIGNER
(Jupiter) (continued)

Characteristics	Suggested character
Very thick	Dogged and determined
Short	Lacks stamina and confidence
Very short	Self-effacing, frightened of the outside world
Very thin	Will succeed in imagination but not in reality
Crooked	Unscrupulous, determined to get their own way regardless of the consequences
Phalanges marked with deep straight vertical lines ("tired lines")	Indication of overwork and fatigue
Curved in a bow toward second finger	Acquisitiveness. Can range from collecting as a hobby if the curve is slight to hoarding and miserliness if the curve is pronounced

THE SECOND OR MIDDLE FINGER (Saturn)

Characteristics	Suggested character
Straight, and in good proportion to the other fingers	A prudent and sensible person, with good concentration and an ability to plan ahead, but who needs privacy
Long, strong, and heavy	Serious and thoughtful, likely to have a hard and difficult life
Slightly longer than first and third fingers	Dry, cool, socially withdrawn
Short	Intuitive, unintellectual
Middle phalange longest	Green-fingered, loves the country
Curved	Shows the inclination to the inner or the outer side of life, depending on the direction of the curve
Crooked	Full of self pity
Same length as first and third fingers	Irresponsible
Very long	Morbid, melancholic, pedantic

THE THIRD OR RING FINGER (Apollo)

Characteristics	Suggested character
Strong and smooth	Emotionally balanced
Smooth, with smooth joints	Creative
Long	Conceited, longing for fame
Very long	Introverted
Short	Shy, lacks emotional control
Third phalange longest	Desires money and luxury
Bending toward second finger	Anxiety-ridden, always on the defensive
Second and third fingers bending together	Secretive
Nail phalange bending toward second finger	Afflictions of the heart—these may be emotional or physical
Bending or drooping toward palm when hand is relaxed	Difficulty coming to terms with intuitive aspects of personality
Crooked or distorted	Emotional difficulties

THE FOURTH OR LITTLE FINGER (Mercury)

Characteristics	Suggested character
Reaching above top crease on third finger	Highly intelligent, fluent, expressive, good business ability
Reaching nail on third finger	Untrustworthy
Short	Difficulty in making the best of oneself
Long first phalange	Knowledgeable, considerable interest in education
First phalange very much longer than others	Tends to exaggerate or to embroider the truth
Short or almost non-existent third phalange.	Degeneracy
Bending toward third finger	Shrewd, clever in business and at making money
Bent toward palm when hand is relaxed	Sexual difficulties
Twisted or crooked	Dishonest, a liar, uses questionable business practices

THE THUMB

Unlike the fingers, the thumb bears no god's name, but is sometimes linked to the first house of the horoscope. It is a key indicator of the level of vitality or life energy and is almost as important to a reading as all the fingers put together, according to some palmists.

Thumb characteristics and meanings

Characteristic	Suggested character traits
Long	A good leader, clear-minded, willpower tempered by good judgment
Very long	Tyrannical, despotic, determined to get own way
Short	Impressionable, indecisive, with the heart ruling the head
Large	Capable and forceful
Short and thick	Obstinate
Small and weak	Lacking in energy and willpower
Straight and stiff	Reserved, loyal, reliable, cautious, stubborn
Flexible	A flexible nature, easy-going, generous, tolerant, tends to be extravagant

The phalanges of the thumb

The phalanges of the thumb each have traditional associations—the first (bearing the nail) with the will, the second with logic. The third is the pad of flesh that frames one side of the palm. Traditionally, this is read with the other similarly prominent pads on the hand, which are known as mounts.

Characteristics	Suggested character traits
Smooth joints	Full of vitality
Knotty joints	Energy comes in erratic bursts
High set	Acquisitive, mean
Low set	Courageous, versatile
Lies close to palm	Not quite honest
Bent, hidden under fingers	Unhappy and self-destructuve
Forming clear right angle to palm when outstretched	A strong sense of justice
Forming an angle greater than a right angle	Too tender-hearted

Thumb phalanges: characteristics and meanings

Characteristic	Suggested character traits
Equal length (a)	Well-balanced personality
Full thumb—first and second of fairly even width (b)	Blunt, outspoken
Broad and sturdy first	Plenty of stamina and well-directed energy
First longer than the second	Energy uncontrolled by logic
Clubbed first (c)	Violent, full of uncontrolled energy. Traditionally the "murderer's thumb"

MOUNTS

In palmistry, the fleshy parts of the palm are called "mounts." There are eight of these, the characteristics of which may help form part of your reading. The base of the thumb, its third phalange, is called the mount of Venus. This phalange brings emotional matters to join will and logic in the thumb's overall frame of reference. Areas nearer the thumb are concerned with our relationships with the outside world, and those farther away with inner matters. The mount of the moon is a pad of flesh opposite the thumb. It reflects both lunar folklore and astrological references in its connection

Characteristic	Suggested character traits
Very tapered first	Lacks stamina and vitality
Broad and sturdy second	Logical, thoughtful, thinks before acting
Second longer than first	Inhibited, feels restricted
Waisted second (**d**)	Quick-thinking, tactful, impulsive, can be evasive

with intuitive, imaginative, even mystic mental activity. Other mounts are located at the base of the fingers and share the same names as the fingers. These mounts usually counterbalance or reinforce what the fingers reveal. Personality clues can also come from a blurring of the boundaries between the mounts.

The god of war—Mars—does not give his name to any of the fingers, but to two mounts on the hand, the upper and lower mounts of Mars. The lower is linked with physical courage and aggression, the upper with moral courage and resistance.

Mount of Venus (1)

Characteristics	Suggested character
Broad, firm, and rounded	Healthy, warmhearted, sincere, compassionate, loves children.
Flat, underdeveloped	Delicate constitution, detached and self-contained nature.
Large	A high degree of vitality.
Very large, overdeveloped	Extremely energetic physically, hedonistic.
High and firm	Highly sexed.
High and soft	Excitable and fickle.
Lower part of mount more prominent	Energy probably channeled into artistic concerns.
Marked with a large saltire	A person who has only one great love in their life.

Lower mount of Mars (2)

Characteristics	Suggested character
Normal size	Physically brave, resolute, able to keep a cool head in a crisis.
Flat, underdeveloped	Cowardly, afraid of physical suffering.
Very large, overdeveloped	Violent, argumentative, possibly cruel, never afraid of taking risks.

Mounts

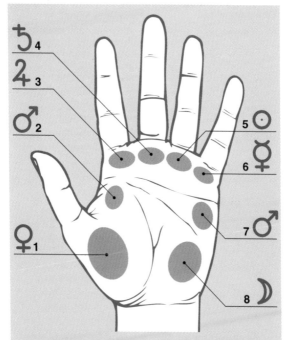

1 Mount of Venus
2 Lower mount of Mars
3 Mount of Jupiter
4 Mount of Saturn
5 Mount of Apollo
  (mount of the Sun)
6 Mount of Mercury
7 Upper mount of Mars
8 Mount of the Moon

Mount of Jupiter (3)

Characteristics	Suggested character
Normal size	Enthusiastic, ambitious, good-tempered, friendly. Self-confident and generous. Conventional and conservative at heart, a lover of pomp and ritual.
Flat, underdeveloped	Selfish, lazy, inconsiderate, lacks confidence.
Very large, overdeveloped	Arrogant, overbearing, self-centered, driven by ambition.
Connected with the mount of Saturn	Happier working in partnership than alone.

Mount of Saturn (4)

Characteristics	Suggested character
Normal size	Introspective, serious-minded, studious, prudent.
Flat, underdeveloped	A run-of-the-mill person with an unremarkable destiny.
Very large, overdeveloped	Gloomy, withdrawn, a recluse. Possibly morbid and suicidal.
Leaning toward the mount of Jupiter	A solemn person who aims high.
Leaning toward the mount of Apollo	Intense appreciation of beauty.

Mount of Apollo (Mount of the Sun) (5)

Characteristics	Suggested character
Normal size	Pleasant, sunny nature, with a lucky streak. Has good taste and artistic leanings.
Flat, underdeveloped	Leads a dull, aimless existence, with no interest in art or culture.
Very large, overdeveloped	Pretentious, extravagant, hedonistic.
Leaning toward the mount of Mercury	Able to make money from the arts.
Connected with the mount of Mercury	Any introvert or extrovert tendencies shown in the fingers will be reinforced.

Mount of Mercury (6)

Characteristics	Suggested character
Normal size	Lively, persuasive, hard-working, needs variety and company.
Flat, underdeveloped	Dull, gullible, humorless. A failure.
Large	Good sense of humor.
Very large, overdeveloped	A sharp conman, materialistic and light-fingered, a cheat.
Marked by short, straight lines	Caring, compassionate, a potential healer.

Upper mount of Mars (7)

Characteristics	Suggested character
Normal size	Morally courageous.
Flat, underdeveloped	Cowardly, interested only in self-preservation.
Very large, overdeveloped	Bad-tempered, sarcastic, mentally cruel.

Mount of the Moon (8)

Characteristics	Suggested character
Normal size	Sensitive, perceptive, romantic, imaginative, artistic, possibly with great love of the sea.
Flat, underdeveloped	Unimaginative, unsympathetic, unstable, cold, bigoted.
Very large, overdeveloped	Overimaginative, introspective, probably untruthful.
High and firm	Creative, with a powerful and fertile imagination.
High and soft	Touchy, thin-skinned, fickle, dreamer.
Reaching to the mount of Venus	Extremely passionate.
Reaching toward the wrist	Supposed to indicate the possession of occult powers.

LINES

On nearly every hand there appear three major lines—
the head-, the heart-, and the lifelines—plus many other
minor lines. It is necessary to take into account the
meanings of these various lines if you want to make a
complete and rounded reading.

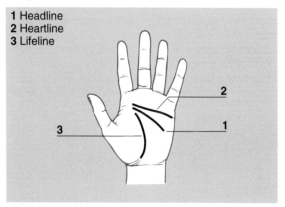

1 Headline
2 Heartline
3 Lifeline

Headline

This is concerned with our mental attitudes and should
be related to the shape of the hand. For example, a
sloping headline on a sensitive hand acts as a
confirmation of the imaginative nature of the subject,
whereas a sloping headline on a practical hand would
be unusual—you would normally expect to find a
straight headline on a practical hand—and might
suggest a person who uses their imagination in a
practical way, perhaps as a designer or inventor.

Reading a headline

Characteristics	Fortune & character
Straight across palm (**1**)	Practical, realistic, down-to-earth, a good organizer.
Sloping toward mount of the Moon (**2**)	Sensitive, imaginative.
Long, reaching top part of mount of the Moon (**3**)	Talent for self-expression.
Starts just touching the lifeline (**4**)	Prudent, moderate, balanced.
Starts with a small separation from lifeline (**5**)	Independent, enterprising, in need of definite direction to prevent wasting energy on trivia.

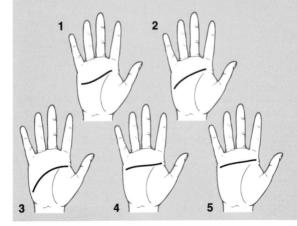

Characteristics	Fortune & character
Starts with a wide separation from lifeline (6)	Foolhardy, excitable.
Starts linked to lifeline for some distance (7)	Very cautious, needs encouragement, responds badly to criticism.
Starts inside lifeline on mount of Mars (8)	Touchy, irritable.
Ends with a large fork that touches both the mount of the Moon and the heartline (9)	Able to be subsumed in another's personality, will give up everything for love.
Straight, ends with a small fork pointing to the mount of the Moon (10)	Imagination restrained by common sense.

Reading a headline (continued)

Characteristics	Fortune & character
Ends in a large fork (**11**)	Too versatile, unable to achieve excellence in any one thing.
Ending in a three-pronged fork (**12**)	Combines intelligence, imagination, and business ability.
Branchline to mount of Jupiter (**13**)	Ambitious and successful.
Branchline to mount of Saturn (**14**)	Ambitious, but will have to struggle for success.
Branchline to mount of Apollo (**15**)	Achieving success through use of own talents.

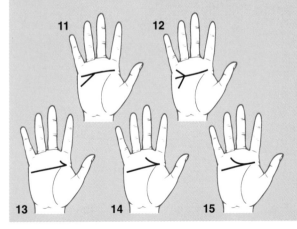

Characteristics	Fortune & character
Long and straight	Shrewd, good forward planner, good memory.
Long, reaching lower part of mount of the Moon	Overimaginative.
Running toward center of wrist	Out of touch with reality.
Curving up toward heartline	Good business ability, good at making money.
Running close to heartline	Narrow in outlook.
Weak, and some distance from lifeline	A tendency to gamble.
Clear and distinct	Good concentration.
Chain-like appearance	Poor concentration, scatterbrained.
Break in the line	A traumatic event with far-reaching effect on mental attitudes.
Discontinuities in the line	Changes in mental attitudes but less traumatic.
Long, sloping end with a fork	Clever, diplomatic, talent for self-expression.

Reading a headline (continued)

Characteristics	Fortune & character
Ends in mount of Mercury	Very good at making money—has the Midas touch.
Branchline ending between third and fourth fingers	Successful scientist or inventor.
Branchline to mount of Mercury	Successful in business

The length of the line indicates the level of intelligence, breadth of understanding, and use made of intellectual potential. The longer the line, the greater the importance played by intellectual matters.

Heartline

This is concerned with our emotions and should be referred to other indicators of our feelings, the finger of Mercury and the mount of Venus.

Reading a heartline

Characteristics	Fortune & character
Long, generously curved, some distance from the bases of the fingers	Warmhearted, sensual, demonstrative.
Longer and stronger than headline	The heart rules the head.
Straight	Reserved and self-interested.
Short and faint	A limited capacity for love.

Reading a heartline (continued)

Characteristics	Fortune & character
Very long, deep, close to the fingers	Possessive, jealous.
Chain-like appearance	A flirt.
Blurred appearance	Tendency to emotional difficulties.
Broken in several places	Unfaithful, lacks constancy.
Broken under second finger	Jilted.
Broken under third finger	A jilt.
Broken sections overlapping	A temporary separation.
Starts between fingers of Saturn and Jupiter	A relationship that involves friendship as well as love.
Chain-like appearance and starting on mount of Saturn	Contempt for the opposite sex.
Starts at same point as headline and lifeline	Extremely selfish, lacks control over emotions.
Running together with headline as one line	Known as the "simian line." A sign of enormous internal struggle, possibly of mental handicap.
Branchline running to fateline	A romance, if the branchline does not touch the fateline; an unhappy marriage if they cross.

continued

Reading a heartline (continued)

Characteristics	Fortune & character
Many small branches (**1**)	A vivid, dynamic personality. Each branch is supposed to represent a dynamic attachment, pointing upward for those that are successful and downward for those that are not.
Starts in middle mount of Jupiter (**2**)	Fussy, discriminating when choosing friends and lovers, extremely loyal to those chosen. Seeks to marry well.
Starts with a fork on mount of Jupiter (**3**)	Lovable, easy to live with, makes a good marriage partner.
Starts with a large fork, one prong on mount of Jupiter (**4**)	Changeable, moody, difficulty living with others.
Starts on mount of Saturn (**5**)	Sensual, but lacking real depth of feeling for others.
Branchline running to headline (**6**)	A partner met through work, or a marriage that is a working partnership.

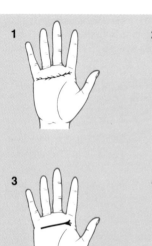

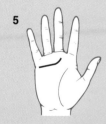

Lifeline

This does not indicate how long a subject will live but shows the strength of a person's vitality—their "life energy"—and so it should be read in conjunction with

Reading a lifeline

Characteristics	Fortune & character
Starts on mount of Jupiter (**1**)	Highly ambitious, likely to succeed.
Starts from headline (**2**)	Controlled and calculating.
Starts well below headline (**3**)	Lacks control, uninhibited.
Two small branches from beginning of line onto headline (**4**)	An inheritance: could be money, but more likely to have been given a good start in life by parents.
Branchline to headline from halfway down line (**5**)	Success and recognition will come in middle age.
Branchline to mount of Apollo (**6**)	Talents will be recognized and rewarded.
Long and clear	Good vitality, a healthy constitution.
Short and checkered	Lacks energy, may be physically frail.
Chain-like appearance	Alternating enthusiasm and torpor, energy coming uneasily in fits and starts.

continued

the thumb, the finger of Jupiter, and the mount of
Venus, which are also important in this area.

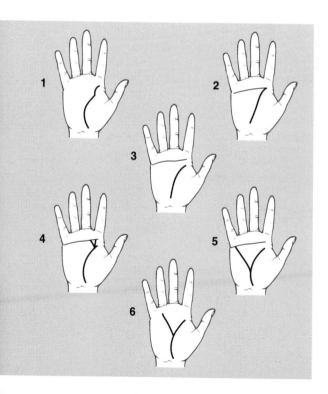

Reading a lifeline (continued)

Characteristics	Fortune & character
Discontinuities in the line	Changes in the direction of life.
Break in the line on one hand only	An illness, followed by a speedy recovery.
Break in the line on both hands	A more serious illness.
Many small branches running upward	Good health, prosperity.
Many small branches running downward	Poor health, financial setbacks.
Ends in a fork with one branch ending in the mount of the Moon	Indicates long-distance travel.
Branchline to mount of Jupiter	Self-confident and self-assured.
Branchline to mount of Saturn	Life will be a struggle, must make own way without outside help.
Branchline to mount of Moon	A longing for a new stimulus, for change. Traditionally, a sea journey.

Line of fate

This line relates to our destiny.

Reading a line of fate

Characteristics	Fortune & character
No line	A smooth and uneventful life.
Straight and unbroken	A successful, untroubled life.
Starts from lifeline (**1**)	Hampered by early environment and family surroundings. Point of separation of lines shows when independence was or will be achieved.
Starts from top bracelet (**2**)	Early responsibilty.
Starts from mount of Venus, ends on mount of Saturn (**3**)	A secure and loved childhood, supported by parents and family. Possibly success through inheritance.

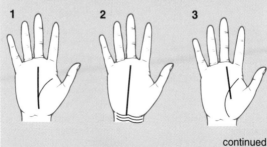

continued

Reading the line of fate (continued)

Characteristics	Fortune & character
Chain-like sections	Unhappy periods in life.
Wavy	Argumentative, changeable, disorganized.
Break in the line	Sudden change in circumstances.
Broken sections overlapping	Planned major changes.
Short bar across line	Setback or obstacle.
Reaching mount of Saturn	Trying to exceed own powers.
Curved toward mount of Jupiter	Success through effort.
Starts from headline to heartline	Success late in life.
Starts from mount of the Moon	A varied life, much traveling.
Ends on headline	Prone to errors of judgment, bad planning leads to misfortune.
Ends on heartline	Sacrifices necessary in the cause of love or duty.
Ends on mount of Apollo	Popular and talented.
Branchline to line of Apollo	Successful partnership. If the lines cross, partnership will fail.
Branchline to mount of Mercury	Achievement and wealth obtained through business or science.

Line of the Sun (Apollo)

This line relates to our good fortune, and to our creativity.

Reading the line of the Sun (Apollo)

Characteristics	Fortune & character
Clear and straight	A lucky person with a charming and sunny nature.
Blurred	Lacks concentration, wastes effort.
Starts close to wrist between mounts of Venus and the Moon, ends in mount of the Sun (**1**)	Nothing ever goes wrong in this life.
Starts with headline (**2**)	Success in middle age as a result of own efforts.
Starts from heartline (**3**)	Warmth, happiness, and sufficiency in old age.

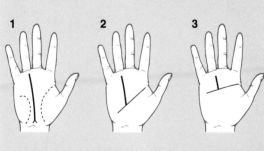

continued

Reading the line of the Sun (continued)

Characteristics	Fortune & character
Starts from life or fateline, ends in mount of the Sun	Success as a result of using talents and energy.
Ends in many small lines	Unsettled, with many conflicting interests.
Starts from mount of Venus (**4**)	Artistically gifted.
Starts from mount of the Moon (**5**)	Strongly attractive to the opposite sex, a person idolized by the masses.
Ends in a fork with prongs on mounts of Mercury, Saturn, and Apollo (**6**)	Lasting success on a firm base.
No line	A life of disappointments and setbacks, however talented the owner of the hand.

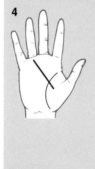

Minor lines

The girdle of Venus relates to passion, the Via Lasciva (Milky Way) to desires, the Rascettes (bracelets) to health, wealth and travel. The lines of health, marriage and children all have their own spheres of influence.

1 Girdle of Venus
2 Hepatica (line of health)
3 Via Lasciva
4 Child lines
5 Rascettes (bracelets)
6 Line of Mars (the inner lifeline)
7 Lines of marriage

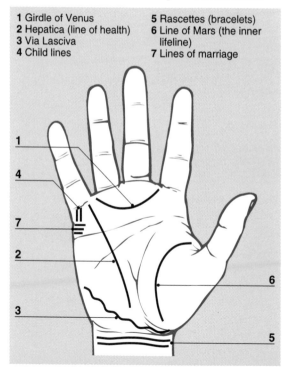

Reading the girdle of Venus

Characteristics	Suggested character
No line	A well-controlled, calm personality.
Well-marked	Overemotional, craves excitement and variety.
Short	Keenly aware of the feelings of others.
Blurred or broken	Oversensitive.
Crosses lines of fate and the Sun	Witty, talented.
Ends on mount of Mercury	Enormous reserves of energy, but a tendency to go to extremes.
Runs off side of the hand instead of making a semicircle	Vacillating, a ditherer.

Reading hepatica (the line of health)

Characteristics	Suggested character
No line	A strong and healthy constitution.
Deeply engraved	Low physical resistance.
Wavy	Digestive problems.
Blurred	Lack of physical stamina.
Touches lifeline	Take extra care of heart at that time.

Reading the Via Lasciva (Milky Way)

Characteristics	Suggested character
Straight	Restless, easily bored.
Straight and long, reaching mount of Mercury	An eloquent speaker of dubious morality.
Curved	A person who is his or her own worst enemy.
Curved, and beginning inside mount of Venus	Liable to take things to excess. Someone who could easily become addicted—to drugs, alcohol, etc.
Branchline reaching to line of the Sun	Potential riches if lines do not quite touch. Financial losses as the result of a relationship (e.g., an expensive divorce settlement) if they cross.

Reading child lines

Characteristics	Suggested character
When present	The lines run from the base of the finger of Mercury to the marriage lines. The number of lines are said to indicate the number of children, with the stronger lines representing boys, and the fainter lines girls.

Reading the rascettes (bracelets)

Characteristics	Suggested character
Parallel and clearly marked	A healthy, wealthy, long and peaceful life.
Chain-like top bracelet	Eventual happiness after a difficult life.
Top bracelet arching into the palm of a woman's hand	Possible difficulties in childbirth.
Line from top bracelet to mount of Jupiter	A long and profitable journey.
Line from top bracelet to mount of the Sun	A trip to a hot country.
Line from top bracelet to mount of Mercury	Sudden wealth.
Lines from top bracelet to mount of the Moon	Each line represents a journey.

Reading the line of Mars (the inner lifeline)

Characteristics	Suggested character
When present	Sustains life in times of illness or danger.

Reading the lines of marriage

Characteristics	Suggested character
Strongly marked	A marriage or close relationship. The number of lines is supposed to indicate the number of such relationships.
Weakly marked	Each line indicates a minor romantic attachment of little importance.
Long and straight	A long and happy relationship.
Broken	Divorce or separation.
Broken lines overlapping	A reunion after a separation, perhaps remarriage to the same person.
Double line	A relationship with two people at the same time, the relative depths of the relationships being indicated by the strength of the lines.
Curves downward	Will outlive partner.
Strong curve upward to base of little finger	Staying unmarried but not celibate.

continued

Reading the lines of marriage (continued)

Characteristics	Suggested character
Curve upward to line of the Sun	A marriage to a famous or wealthy person if the lines do not quite touch. If the lines cross, the marriage will be unhappy.
Starts with a fork	Delay or frustration at the start of a relationship.
Ends in a fork	A divorce or separation.
Crossed by a line running from base of finger of Mercury	Opposition to a relationship.
Crossed by girdle of Venus	An unhappy marriage, a nagging partner.

FINGERPRINTS

Fingerprints are useful in the detection of personality. Established about 18 weeks after conception, they are unlike other lines on the hand, in that they are fixed and unchanging. Different characteristics will be blended in the subject's personality when more than one type of fingerprint pattern is observed. The number of fingers involved provides clues to that blend. For example, a person with several fingers showing low arches is likely to be far more insensitive than a subject with just one!

Reading fingerprints

Characteristics	Suggested character
Low arch (**a**)	Hard-hearted, insensitive, sceptical, unemotional, and materialistic.
Tented arch (**b**)	Highly strung, artistic, impulsive but stubborn.
Loop (**c**)	Mild-tempered, straightforward, with a quick, lively, and versatile mind.
Whorl (**d**)	An individualist with a strong, definite personality. Potentially brilliant, best when self-employed.
Mixed (**e**)	Mixed-up, muddle-headed personality.

MARKS AND TEXTURES ON THE HAND

Mark	Indicates
Chaining (**a**)	Indecision, weakness, tendency to be unlucky.
Forked line (**b**)	Divisions of interest, contradictions.
Doubled line (**c**)	Strengthening and reinforcing.
Island (**d**)	Period of stress, weakness, breakdown.
Break (**e**)	Unpleasant interruption in the progress of life.
Bar (**f**)	A barrier, opposition.
Cross (**g**)	An upheaval or shock. If at the end of a line, failure.
Star (**h**)	Sudden happenings which may be triumphant or tragic. A hand with many stars indicates an exciting life.
Square (**i**)	A sign of protection, positive and good qualities triumphing over the bad and negative.
Triangle (**j**)	Good fortune, peace, harmony.
Trident (**k**)	Good fortune.
Grille (**l**)	Uncertaintly, lack of direction, confusion.
Spot (**m**)	A temporary cessation.
Circle (**n**)	A rare sign. Similar to the island sign except when found on the line of the Sun or mount of Apollo where it represents the sun and may bring good fortune.

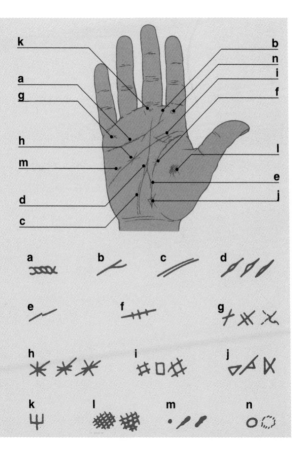

INFLUENCE LINES

Line	Significance
Starting from mount of the Moon and meeting line of fate (**a**)	A close relationship or marriage.
If the influence line is the stronger of the two	The subject's partner will also be the stronger.
Starting from mount of Venus and ending on lifeline (**b**)	Someone who is greatly influenced by people he or she loves.
Curved parallel to lifeline (**c**)	Each of the lines is said to represent a person who will have a great influence on the subject's life.

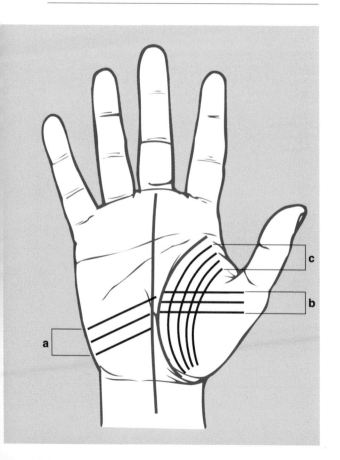

TIMESCALES

It is impossible to make accurate predictions as to
when an event may or may not occur. However, using
timescales it is possible to make a reasonably accurate
guess. The illustrations below show approximate
timescales for the lifeline (**a**), line of fate (**b**), and line of
the Sun (**c**).

a Lifeline
b Line of fate
c Line of the Sun

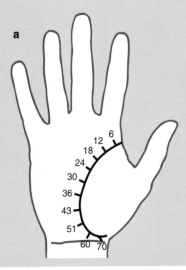

Dates of romantic relationships can be approximated
by examining the distance between the marriage lines
and the heartline; the closer to the base of the fingers
and the farther from the heartline, the later the
marriage.

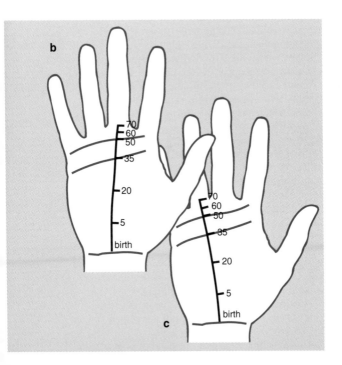

PHRENOLOGY

Definition Assessing character from bumps on the head.

History The theory of phrenology was first put forward in Vienna by Dr. Franz Joseph Gall, in 1796. Dr. Gall argued that thinking affects the shape of our brain, which in turn affects the shape of our skull. He suggested that irregularities in the skull surface, called "bumps," "faculties," or "organs," could be used to evaluate a person's character. Dr. Gall had classified 42 separate faculties by the middle of the nineteenth century when phrenology was at its height. Each of Gall's faculties was supposed to correspond to a facet of personality.

Modern methods Phrenology is no longer a popular form of prediction although it can still be practiced in much the same way as that suggested by Dr. Gall.

Equipment No equipment is necessary although it is often useful to refer to charts such as those shown here, or to models, many of which have become collectors' pieces.

Reading a head

It is not easy to identify all the details of a skull and you will find that your assessments become more accurate only with considerable practice.

1 Consider the overall shape of the head and consult the chart for an overall impression of the person you are assessing.

2 Run your fingertips over the head of your subject,

pressing gently but firmly. Feel all the contours of the skull, checking both sides.

3 Using the charts provided, make an assessment of the character of your subject. Remember to always take an overall view.

Overall head shape	Character traits
Rounded	Strong, confident, courageous, sometimes restless
Square	Solid, reliable, deeply thoughtful and purposeful
Wide	Energetic, outgoing
Narrow	Withdrawn, inward-looking
Ovoid	An intellectual or "egghead"

Interpreting your reading

If a faculty is well developed in comparison to the others, this indicates that this particular quality is present to a considerable degree in the personality; if underdeveloped, this quality is lacking in the personality. For example, a well-developed organ of alimentiveness indicates a person who enjoys food and wine; overdevelopment suggests a glutton who may drink to excess, while underdevelopment indicates a light and finicky eater.

Interpreting your reading

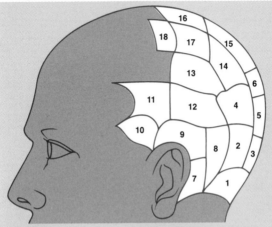

Faculty	Character traits
1 Amativeness	Interest in the opposite sex, sex appeal
2 Conjugality	Capacity for constant, faithful love, the desire for marriage
3 Philopro- genitiveness	Capacity for parental love, filial affection, and care of the less fortunate
4 Adhesiveness	Capacity for affection, friendship, sociability
5 Inhabitiveness	Love of one's home, patriotism

Faculty	Character traits
6 Continuity	The ability to concentrate, to give a subject continuous attention, to make reasoned connections
7 Vitativeness	The love of life, ability to resist ill health
8 Combativeness	Capacity for courage, assertiveness, resistance
9 Execution	Executive capabilities, the power to endure
10 Alimentiveness	The appetitie, love of food
11 Acquisitiveness	The desire to accumulate, the capacity for thrift
12 Secretiveness	Capacity for reserve and discretion
13 Cautiousness	Capacity for being careful
14 Approbativeness	The desire for popularity
15 Self-esteem	Self-confidence, the desire for authority
16 Firmness	Willpower, endurance, and determination
17 Conscientiousness	Integrity and moral discrimination
18 Hopefulness	Optimism

Interpreting your reading (continued)

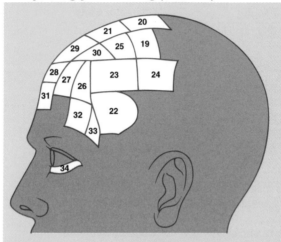

Faculty	Character traits
19 Spirituality	Capacity for religious faith, intuition, psychic abilities
20 Veneration	Respect for society, its rules and institutions
21 Benevolence	Generosity and sympathy
22 Constructiveness	Mechanical and practical ability
23 Ideality	Aesthetic qualities, the love of beauty and perfection

Faculty	Character traits
24 Sublimity	The love of the grand concept and the great creation in both nature and art
25 Imitativeness	Capacity for mimicry, drama, social skills
26 Mirthfulness	Cheerfulness, sense of humor
27 Causality	Thinking and reasoning ability, capacity for planning and deduction
28 Comparison	Ability to form analytical judgments
29 Humanity	Ability to judge people's characters and motives
30 Agreeableness	Capacity for persuasiveness and verbal dexterity
31 Eventuality	Memory for facts, events, and experiences
32 Time	Capacity for judging rhythm, tempo, and timing, for punctuality and for remembering dates
33 Tune	The "ear for music"
34 Language	Ability to learn foreign languages, capacity for eloquence in writing and speaking

Interpreting your reading (continued)

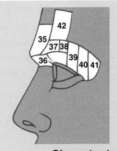

Faculty	Character traits
35 Individuality	The inquisitive mind, the ability to be discriminating and to apply what has been observed
36 Form	Visual skills and memory
37 Size	Ability to judge proportions, sizes, and measurements
38 Weight	Good balance, judgment of weights
39 Color	Skill in blending and using colors
40 Order	The ability to be organized, systematic, and tidy
41 Calculation	Mathematical ability
42 Locality	Sense of place and direction, enjoyment of travel

Examples of characters types

The book *Heads and Faces, and How to Study Them; A Manual of Phrenology and Physiognomy for the People*, by Nelson Sizer and Dr. H. S. Drayton encouraged employers and employees to locate certain faculties and to learn to distinguish between different types of character according to the principles of phrenology.

Reading head shapes

a Idiot
b Malefactor
c Poet

d Criminal
e Moral in character

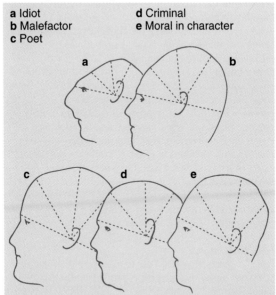

PHYSIOGNOMY

Definition Character analysis using facial features.

History The first systematic account of physiognomy is attributed to Aristotle, although it may have been practiced by Pythagoras, Socrates, and Hippocrates. Early physiognomists compared men and animals and drew analogies about their temperaments based on overall facial appearances. In the sixteenth century, they began to consider individual facial features, and based their character assessment on the shape of eyes, noses, chins, etc. Between the sixteenth and eighteenth centuries, physiognomy flourished, but was received differently in different countries. In some places, physiognomy was accepted as a special science and physiognomists were revered as learned scholars, but in other places they were tortured as heretics.

Modern methods Many people already unwittingly practice physiognomy when they assess a person's character from facial expressions and other mannerisms. In addition to the overall generalizations many of us make when meeting a person for the first time, you can try your hand at physiognomy by using the charts provided here for different facial features.

Equipment Equipment is not required for physiognomy.

Reading faces

Use the charts provided here to assess your subject's character based on face shape, profile, and individual facial features.

Reading face shapes

There are six basic face shapes, shown here with
their predicted character traits.

Shape	Predicted character traits
Round or oval 	<ul><li>Friendly</li><li>Intuitive</li><li>Good judgment</li><li>Definite values</li><li>Strong sense of justice</li><li>Good homemaker</li><li>Loves comfort and luxury</li><li>Capable and hard-working in business</li><li>Can be lazy and self-indulgent</li></ul>
Triangular or heart-shaped 	<ul><li>Tries to make dreams come true</li><li>Can be impractical</li><li>Quick-thinker</li><li>Intellectual</li><li>Good memory</li><li>Can be moody</li><li>Sensitive</li><li>Introspective</li><li>Easily bored</li><li>Needs a sense of purpose</li></ul>

Reading face shapes

Shape	Predicted character traits
Square or rectangular	• A natural leader • Dynamic • Thorough • Always needs to be active • Intelligent • Practical • Mechanically skillful • Physically strong • Strong-willed • Has firm, decided opinions
Round-triangular composite	• Good intellect • Sound commercial sense • Ingenious • Optimistic • Self-confident • Can be complacent • Lacks judgment
Triangular-square composite	• Versatile • Quick-thinking • Translates ideas into actions • Profits from experience • Impetuous
Square-round composite	• Active • Jolly • Happy-go-lucky • Businesslike • Self-interested • Opinionated

Reading profiles

Shape	Predicted character traits
Convex 	<ul><li>Enthusiastic</li><li>Quick-thinker</li><li>Practical</li><li>Sharp witted</li><li>Active</li><li>A talker</li><li>Can be impatient</li><li>Poor listener</li><li>Lacks concentration</li></ul>
Vertical 	<ul><li>Calm</li><li>Reasonable</li><li>An enquiring mind</li><li>Always looking for the best</li><li>Rarely admits failure</li><li>Can be stubborn</li><li>Can be self-opinionated</li></ul>
Concave 	<ul><li>Loyal</li><li>Capable</li><li>Good memory</li><li>Reserved</li><li>Sometimes moody</li><li>Can appear deep-thinking and concerned with major issues while actually being shallow and engrossed in trivia</li></ul>

Reading foreheads

Shape	Predicted character traits
High	Intellectual
High and wide	Philosophical
High and narrow	Analytical
Low	Practical, direct
Convex	Observant
Flat	Deliberate, good concentration
Concave	A good listener, cautious

Reading eyes

Shape	Predicted character traits
Round	Naive, trusting
Oval	Shrewd, good-humored
Slanting	Secretive, self-indulgent
Wide open	Confident, friendly
Hooded	Scheming, envious
Narrowed	Keen, suspicious
Wide apart	Confident, broad-minded
Close together	Responsible, narrow-minded
Protuberant	Smooth talker, full of repartee
Deep set	Slow-talking, sticks to facts
Neither protuberent nor deep set	A convincing speaker and a good listener

Reading eyebrows

Shape	Predicted character traits
Heavy (**a**)	Intense, blunt
Thin (**b**)	Fastidious, fussy
Straight (**c**)	Alert, active
Curved	Inquiring, curious
Arched (**d**)	Imaginative
Sloping up	Ambitious
Slopping down	Petulant, resigned
Wide apart (**e**)	Adaptable, easily influenced
Close together (**f**)	Full of nervous energy

Reading noses

Shape	Predicted character traits
Large	Aggressive, worldly
Small	Quiet, unassuming
Thin	Nervous, irritable
Wide	Exuberant, careless
Long	Careful, worried
Short	Cheerful
High-bridged, pointed	Vigorous, inquisitive
Straight	Steady, thorough, regimented
Short and snub	Friendly, secretive, plodding

Reading mouths

Shape	Predicted character traits
Large	Generous, extravagant
Small	Selfish, miserly
Curving up	Cheerful
Curving down	Discontented
Large lips	Hedonistic
Narrow lips	Unemotional
Straight lips (a)	Self-controlled
Curved lips (b)	Changeable
Protruding upper lip	Critical, tends to exaggerate
Protruding lower lip	Considerate, pleasant
Lips even in profile	Restrained, assertive, analytical

a   b

Reading chins

Shape	Predicted character traits
Long	Stubborn
Short	Changeable
Pointed	Enthusiastic
Cleft	Self-centered
Double chin	Amiable, self-indulgent
Receding	Argumentative, impatient, trivial
Blunt	Firm, almost stolid, a calm surface hiding a quick temper
Jutting forward	Deliberate, purposeful, and stubborn

Reading ears

Shape	Predicted character traits
Large	Intellectual
Small	Instinctive
Longer than they are wide	Keen, impractical.
Wider than they are long	Very practical
Pointed	Artful, conniving
Large lobes	Independent, strong-minded
Small lobes	Dependent, lacks initiative
No lobes	Unresponsive, lacks sense of purpose
Set close to head	Plans ahead, thrifty
Sticking out	An original thinker

PYROMANCY

Definition Divination by fire. There are many variations, all with different names (see table below).
History Pyromancy played an important part in societies where fire was thought to be a god, or where burnt offerings were made to gods.

Types of pyromancy

Name	Divination by:
Capnomancy	Smoke
Botanomancy	The burning of leaves and branches
Daphnomancy	The burning of laurel leaves
Causinomancy	Objects cast into fire
Halomancy	Casting salt into a fire
Pyroscopy	Burning a sheet of paper on a white surface, and examining the resulting stains
Sideromancy	Casting an odd number of straws onto iron brought to red heat in a fire and reading the omens in the patterns formed by the straws, their movements as they burn, and the nature of the flames and smoke

Modern methods Pictures observed in both the flames and embers of a fire are thought by some to be predictive of future events.

Equipment You can try pyromancy by observing shapes in an ordinary coal fire, for example.

Observing pictures in a fire

1 Scatter a handful of salt over a fire that has died down to a bed of glowing coals.

2 Once the crackling and flames have died down, gaze into the fire. Study any pictures you see there.

3 Concentrate, in silence, for 10–15 minutes. If you see nothing of significance, it is said that the flames have no message for you and you should refrain from another attempt for another 24 hours.

* A shape must stand out clearly from the coals for it to have meaning.
* The more clearly the fire glows, the better the omen is said to be.

Shape	Interpretation
Building	Happiness
Building collapsing	Change in residence or in place of work
Castle	Someone is thinking of you
Cat	Happiness at work
Clover	Great prosperity

continued

Shape	Interpretation
Cow	Someone is thinking of you
Dog	Friendship
Eagle	Warning
Face	If bright, happiness caused by the person whose face is seen; if dull, unhappiness caused by that person
Flowers	Disappointment
Fountain	Happiness
Fruit	If the fruit has been picked, an unhappy love affair; if the fruit is still hanging from the tree, trouble that will pass and be followed by happiness
Hand	If outstretched, someone close to you needs help; if clenched, a surprise
Hatchet	Disaster
Horse	A journey
Lion, tiger, or other wild animal	News from a distance
Mountain	Success

Shape	Interpretation
Pillars	A love affair. Bright pillars indicate the return of a former lover
Ring	One large ring, a wedding ring; two rings, hasty wedding that might prove unfortunate
Sea	If calm, a peaceful life; if troubled, a troubled life
Sheep	Good luck
Ship	A journey
Shoes	Good news
Stair or steps	A wish will be granted, quickly if they are bright; slowly if they are dull and dark
Sword	Danger
Tree	Great success in love or business
Windmill	If bright, change for the better; if dull, change for the worse
Wings	Travel

RUNES

Definition Using symbols of an ancient alphabet to predict the future.

History During the first or second century A.D. the Germanic peoples of Northern Europe began using an alphabet made up of characters called runes. They were used to predict future events, to heal, to control the weather, to protect, and in many other ways. Rune symbols were worn as amulets or talismans and were engraved on swords to improve a warrior's fighting ability.

Modern methods Runes have been used in a similar manner for centuries and can be interpreted using the charts provided here.

Equipment Runes were originally burned or carved into one side of small oblong pieces of wood from a fruit tree, or engraved on copper, bronze or gold disks. Today, you can buy sets of runes in certain specialist shops, but you can make your own rune cards by drawing the runes onto small squares of white board.

Reading runes

1 Scatter the runes face down in front of you.

2 Clear all thoughts from your mind.

3 Ask the enquirer to mix up the runes and—still face down—to arrange 13 of them in a pattern known as the runic wheel.

4 Turn all of the runes face up and begin your interpretation, using the tables provided.

The runic wheel

Each position on the runic wheel is connected with a different aspect of life and these should be taken into account when making your reading.

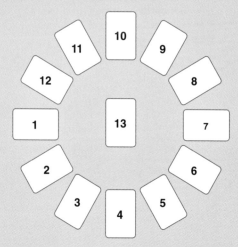

1 The self, the personality
2 Money, possessions
3 Family
4 The home
5 Creativity, self-expression
6 The outside world, physical health
7 Love and marriage
8 Inheritance, death
9 Education, travel
10 Careers, social status
11 Friendships, pleasure
12 The inner life, psychic qualities
13 The enquirer

Rune interpretations

As well as taking into account the aspect of life runes are connected with, each rune should be related to the rune on either side of it, to the rune immediately opposite it, and to the center rune.

Runes are in their upright position (**a**) if their tops face the center of the wheel; the tops of reversed runes (**b**) face the outside of the wheel.

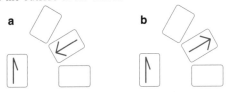

Rune	Position	Interpretation
ᛉ	Upright	Be careful and plan ahead
	Reversed	Impatience will lead to failure
ᚠ	Upright	Romantic fulfillment
	Reversed	Romantic difficulties

Rune	Position	Interpretation
	Upright	Intuition
	Reversed	Be cautious with money
	Upright	Old age, wisdom
	Reversed	Bad advice, senility
	Upright	A passionate love affair
	Reversed	A parting, sadness caused by friends
	Upright	An old problem solved
	Reversed	An old problem causing new difficulties

Rune interpretations

Rune	Position	Interpretation
	Upright	Changes at work
	Reversed	An offer that should be refused
	Upright	Wills, inheritances, legacies
	Reversed	Accidents, damage
	Upright	News, a stranger.
	Reversed	Problems in communication
	Upright	New relationships, partnerships
	Reversed	Loss of a friend

Rune	Position	Interpretation
	Upright	Moving house, crossing water
	Reversed	An unpleasant journey
	Upright	Happiness and success^
	Reversed	Self-sacrifice, delay
	Upright	Holidays, travel, visits
	Reversed	Sudden journeys and changes
	Upright	Family, marriage, fertility, children
	Reversed	Ill health, sterility, divorce

Rune interpretations

Rune	Position	Interpretation
	Upright	Financial good fortune, promotion
	Reversed	A lost opportunity
	Upright	A flash of inspiration
	Reversed	An inability to see the obvious
	Upright	Minor delays and family disagreements
	Reversed	Major delays and family quarrels
	Upright	A gift, windfall, or pleasant surprise
	Reversed	Unreliable confidants

Rune	Position	Interpretation
	Upright	Legal documents, contracts
	Reversed	Enemies
	Upright	Major changes leading to prosperity
	Reversed	Isolation, detachment
	Upright	Certain success
	Reversed	A failure that leads to a new opportunity
		Fate, "karma," the inevitable

SCRYING

Definition Divination by gazing into a reflective surface. Different forms have different names.

History Anything with a reflective surface can be used for scrying. Early forms involved water and other liquids. The Egyptians gazed into a pool of ink in the hand; Babylonians gazed into liquids in sacred bowls; Hindus used bowls of molasses and the Greeks lowered mirrors into sacred fountains and springs. Gazing into a crystal ball (crystallomancy) is another form of scrying, known in Europe since about the fifth century, and used by the Mayans and Incas, by North American Indians and Australian aborigines, and by tribes in Borneo, New Guinea, and Madagasgar. Catoptromancy is a form of scrying involving the use of mirrors, early forms of which were made of polished metal. The ancient Chinese used polished bronze mirrors, decorated with cosmological and astrological symbols, into which they looked for reflections of demons. In the fourteenth century, witches were said to use mirrors of polished onyx to speak to spirits. Catoptromancy reached its height in the late Middle Ages when mirrors were made of silvered glass, like those in use today. One of the most famous seers of all time was Michel de Notredame (1503–1566), better known as Nostradamus, known to have used a brass bowl of water resting on a tripod, as well as a looking glass, for his prophecies.

Modern methods Today, the most popular and widespread form of scrying involves the use of crystal balls.

Equipment All kinds of reflective surfaces have been
used, including precious stones, glass, water, polished
metal, and even blood and soap bubbles. When using a
crystal ball, some crystallomancers use a lamen (**a**).
This is an ornate circular table which stands within a
magic circle (**b**). Both the table and the circle on the
floor are engraved with mystic names. Candles may be
used (**c**), one engraved ELOHIM and the other ELOHE.
The pedestal (**d**) on which the crystal stands is named
SADAY.

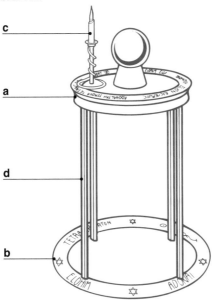

CRYSTALLOGRAPHY

For this type of scrying, use a sphere about 4 in (10 cm) in diameter, made of beryl or quartz crystal. Glass spheres may also be used but should be free from any blemishes or bubbles.

Care of your crystal ball

- Only you should handle your crystal ball.
- Keep the ball away from extremes of hot and cold.
- Do not allow direct sunlight to fall on the ball as this is said to ruin the susceptibility of the crystal. (Moonlight, however, is thought to be beneficial.)
- Wash the ball using vinegar and water only.
- Polish the ball using a velvet cloth or chamois leather.
- Always keep the ball wrapped up when not in use.

Preparing to use the crystal ball

1 Use a north-facing room for your reading.
2 Ensure that there is just enough light to read by.
3 Use a black cloth to aid concentration, placing it on the table or as a curtain behind the crystal.
4 Place the crystal on the table or hold it in your hand. Or, support the crystal on the traditional lamen within its mystic circle of names.
5 Do not allow more than two people in the room with you at any one time. Ask them to sit quietly, at least an arm's length away.

Using the crystal ball

1 Sit still, empty your mind, and gaze into the crystal.
2 The crystal should fill with a milky hue. This should change color and eventually become black.

3 When the blackness rolls away, images are revealed. These may be symbolic shapes and colored clouds. Use the chart (pages 302–303) to interpret them. If you see moving images—like a film—you need only report what you see.

The correct mental attitude

Scrying is said to come easily to only about one person in twenty, so do not worry if at first you are unable to see anything in your crystal. You will need to practice and persevere in order to develop any latent powers. Some crystallographers and catoptromancers use elaborate rituals to prepare themselves and to create the right atmosphere of inner tranquillity and calm. Some people like to use meditation to help prepare and calm the mind. The method that is best suited to you for preparing yourself for any kind of reading is likely to be developed over time.

Interpreting symbols in the crystal

Symbol	Interpretation
Anchor	Safety, hope
Beetle	Long life
Bird	A message
Crown	Glory, responsibility
Eye	Good fortune, forethought, but can be a symbol of evil
Frog	Fertility, something beneficial but hidden
Fruit	Children
Globe	Travel
Heart pierced by a dagger	Suffering
Lighthouse	Danger ahead, but there is hope
Mask	Deceit, tragedy
Scales	Justice, even-handedness—or the reverse
Skull	Death, wisdom
Snake	Health, knowledge, temptation
Star	Success, but be careful
Swords	A quarrel
Waterlily	Creativity

Interpreting clouds in the crystal

Cloud	Interpretation
White	Good fortune
Black	Ill fortune
Violet, green or blue	Joy
Red, orange or yellow	Danger
Ascending clouds	An affirmative reply to your question
Descending clouds	A negative reply to your question
Clouds moving to the right	Spirits present
Clouds moving to the left	Spirits have departed

Interpreting events in the crystal

Event	Interpretation
If at front of crystal	Relates to the present or immediate future
If at back of crystal	Relates to the remote past or distant future
If to your left	Events are real
If to your right	Events are symbolic

SORTILEGE

Definition Divination by the casting or drawing of lots, derived from the Latin, *sors*, the word for lot, and *sortilegus*, meaning diviner. An alternative name for sortilege is cleromancy, from *kleros*, the Greek word for lot.

History There are many types of sortilege. In aleuromancy, answers to a specific question were baked inside small balls of dough (**a**) and chosen at random, thought to have been common practice until the ninth century. Another form of sortilege is astragalomancy, divination by casting small bones called astragals (**b**) (usually the vertebrae or ankle bones of sheep). Belomancy is divination by arrows and probably dates back to the Babylonians. It was also practiced by the Sythians, Arabs, and some North American Indian tribes. Opening a book at random and taking an omen from the first words read—bibliomancy— is another form of sortilege. It is also known as stichomancy: a "stich" is a line of verse or a short section of prose. Divination from a book of poetry is sometimes known as rhapsodomancy. In the late Middle Ages the works of the Roman writer Virgil were the most popular choice, and bibliomancy was known as the *sortes Virgilianae*—the "Virgilian lots."

Modern methods Many of us have unthinkingly determined our future by lots at some time in our lives—drawing straws to select a person to carry out a particular action, for example, or tossing a coin to make a decision. Sweepstakes, lotteries, bingo, roulette, etc., are all forms of gambling that depend on casting or drawing lots. In China, "fortune cookies" are used. These are small hollow pastries which are broken open to reveal a slip of paper that bears the chooser's fortune.

Equipment A huge variety of objects have been used for lots. In Africa, lots could be sacred stones or carved wooden or bone divining sticks—the tradition varies from tribe to tribe. Divining sticks are also known among the North American Indians and in parts of Asia. In Polynesia, a coconut was spun, and answered questions according to how it fell. In Japan, slips of paper inscribed with omens for the future were placed in containers and drawn at random, Pessomancy (psephomancy) is divination by drawing or casting of specially marked pebbles (**c**). Many African witch doctors keep bags of "wise stones" that are cast to foretell the future. Greek lots were specially marked wooden counters, drawn from an urn or cast on the ground, (although the oracle at Delphi used beans as lots).

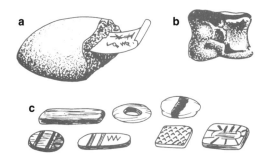

SORTILEGE USING STONES

1 Choose nine small, round-edged stones. You should be able to hold all nine together in your hand.

2 Mark symbols on one side of each stone.

3 Shake the stones in your hand, concentrating on your question, and cast the stones in front of you.

4 Using the chart provided, read only those stones whose symbols are showing.

Symbol	Color	Interpretation
Bird (**a**)	Brown	Communications, visitors
Eye (**b**)	White	"I" the questioner
Fence (**c**)	Black	Delay, restrictions, old age
Flower (**d**)	Blue	Success, prosperity
Moon (**e**)	Gray	The inner life, women
Rings (**f**)	Green	Relationships, harmony
Sun (**g**)	Yellow	Health, the outer life, men
Swords (**h**)	Red	Drive, energy, strife
Waves (**i**)	Blue-green	The intellect, travel

- Events in the near future are represented by symbols on stones close to you; stones farther away foretell the more distant future.
- Stones that touch or that are very close together should be read in conjunction with each other.

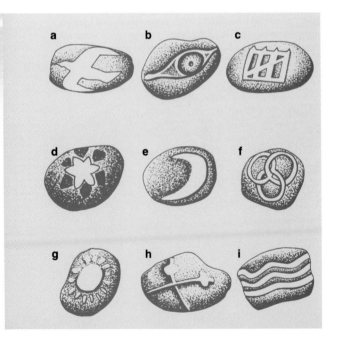

TABLETS OF FATE

Definition Divination which combines the occult significance of numbers with the random element of casting lots.

History The origins of tablets of fate cannot be traced, although they are known to have been popular in the seventeenth century, when they were on sale in the form of cheap pamphlets sold in the street and known as chap books. In the nineteenth century they were used more as parlor games than as a serious means of divination.

Modern methods Tablets of fate are popular among some diviners because they can be devised so that answers have particular relevance to a person's lifestyle. Although experts may differ as to the frequency with which you may ask questions, and the exact rituals employed, all the tablets shown here are used in essentially the same way. Popular tablets include the Sphinx, and tablets for love, home and family, time, justice, work and finance, and travel.

Equipment Modern tablets can be simply made using numbers written onto shapes of paper. It is quite permissible for you to devise your own number sequence and list of answers. You will also need a pencil or pointer.

Using tablets of fate

Consult the tablet of the Sphinx first. This will tell you whether the present moment is suitable for using this method of divination. You may only put your questions to an appropriate tablet if the Sphinx gives a positive answer. It is helpful to have someone else present when you use the tablets.

1 Shut your eyes.

2 Concentrate on the question you wish to ask.

3 If someone else is present, ask him or her to turn the tablet round three times.

4 Using the thumb and forefinger of your left hand, take the pencil by the blunt end and dangle it over the table.

5 The other person present should move the tablet of fate so that it is just under the pencil.

6 Some diviners trace a circle or square in the air three
times, using the pencil.
7 Bring the point down on to the tablet, and open your
eyes.
8 See which number the pencil has come down on and
consult the key to find your answer.

- If the pencil misses the tablet completely three times,
do not try again for at least 24 hours.
- If when you open your eyes the page is upside down,
take the answer given after the word "reversed" in the
key.

Tablet of the Sphinx

This tablet should be consulted first as it tells you
whether the other tablets will give you true answers at
the present time.

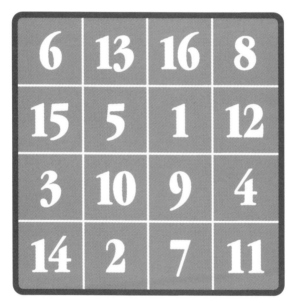

See next page for meanings.

Tablet of the Sphinx: meanings

Number and position of paper	Meaning
1 Upright **1** Reversed	Now is the time to test your fate. Today is not the time.
2 Upright **2** Reversed	Tomorrow will be preferable. Yes, straight away.
3 Upright **3** Reversed	Thursday is the best day. Try any day but Thursday.
4 Upright **4** Reversed	You are too impatient. Leave it as it is.
5 Upright **5** Reversed	Try on Sunday. Not on Sunday.
6 Upright **6** Reversed	Lose no time. Wait one week exactly.
7 Upright **7** Reversed	The answers are waiting. Do not even try.
8 Upright **8** Reversed	Try on Tuesday. Not until next week.
9 Upright **9** Reversed	Try on the day on which you were born. Soon, if you do not lose your temper.

Number and position of paper	Meaning
10 Upright **10** Reversed	Saturday is preferable. No Saturday is suitable.
11 Upright **11** Reversed	There is nothing to say. Secrets wait.
12 Upright **12** Reversed	Monday will be auspicious. Monday is inauspicious.
13 Upright **13** Reversed	Lose no time. First be sure of your own mind.
14 Upright **14** Reversed	Try on Friday. Good fortune awaits you.
15 Upright **15** Reversed	Try on Wednesday. Certainly not.
16 Upright **16** Reversed	Right away. Do not try at all.

Tablet of Venus

This tablet will answer questions connected with love.

5	11	1	9
14	7	4	12
8	3	16	2
6	15	10	13

See opposite for meanings.

Tablet of Venus: meanings

Number and position of paper	Meaning
1 Upright	This love is true.
1 Reversed	Think hard—this person disagrees with you.
2 Upright	Expect some delay.
2 Reversed	Not the kind who is easily deceived.
3 Upright	Follow your heart.
3 Reversed	Flatterers are dangerous.
4 Upright	Yes, if you're sure of your own mind.
4 Reversed	If you knew the truth you'd forgive.
5 Upright	All's well.
5 Reversed	Yours was a hasty judgment.
6 Upright	You will be to blame if you lose this love.
6 Reversed	True love can weather misfortune.
7 Upright	You are causing unhappiness.
7 Reversed	Look beyond appearances.
8 Upright	Do not let jealousy come between you.
8 Reversed	A friend who loves you truly.

Tablet of Venus: meanings (continued)

Number and position of paper	Meaning
9 Upright	You are the only one who is loved.
9 Reversed	You are too fond of amusements.
10 Upright	You are in someone's thoughts now.
10 Reversed	Beware of a flirt.
11 Upright	A passing cloud.
11 Reversed	A misundertanding on both sides.
12 Upright	Someone has had a change of mind.
12 Reversed	Evil tongues, evil minds.
13 Upright	Yes, but not the one you are thinking of.
13 Reversed	You should not act hastily.
14 Upright	What reason is there for doubt?
14 Reversed	It was an infatuation—forget it.
15 Upright	Remember what was said as you parted.
15 Reversed	There is no reason to be jealous.
16 Upright	It is true love.
16 Reversed	Be sensible before it is too late.

Tablet of the Moon

This tablet will answer questions concerning your home, relatives and friends.

See next page for meanings.

Tablet of the Moon: meanings

Number and position of paper	Meaning
1 Upright	**All is well, so be patient.**
1 Reversed	You are your own worst enemy.
2 Upright	**The fault is yours.**
2 Reversed	Less than ever.
3 Upright	**Do not let them worry you.**
3 Reversed	If you can do so with a clear conscience.
4 Upright	**Love will find a way.**
4 Reversed	There'll be none.
5 Upright	**It's a question of jealousy.**
5 Reversed	It may possibly come about.
6 Upright	**You are indulging in fantasy.**
6 Reversed	None if you are discreet.
7 Upright	**A fair woman.**
7 Reversed	Sometimes, but rarely.
8 Upright	**It is most unlikely.**
8 Reversed	Something will occur that improves matters.

Number and position of paper	Meaning
9 Upright	You will be disappointed in this matter.
9 Reversed	You will do more harm than good.
10 Upright	Hasty works will be regretted.
10 Reversed	Do not take any of them into your confidence.
11 Upright	Groundless suspicions.
11 Reversed	Current gossip maligns you.
12 Upright	There is a marvellous friend to help.
12 Reversed	The secret is at risk.
13 Upright	Be content.
13 Reversed	Trust the woman who speaks her mind.
14 Upright	Your neighbor is a true friend.
14 Reversed	It will soon be over.
15 Upright	You will have your wish.
15 Reversed	There is no reason for doubt.
16 Upright	A removal.
16 Reversed	Everything is for the best.

Tablet of the Sun

This tablet answers questions concerning time.

10	3	6	13
8	15	1	5
9	11	7	16
2	14	12	4

See opposite for meanings.

Tablet of the Sun: meanings

Number and position of paper	Meaning
1 Upright **1** Reversed	In six month's time. Wait exactly one week.
2 Upright **2** Reversed	Never. In two weeks.
3 Upright **3** Reversed	It will soon come out. Time will tell.
4 Upright **4** Reversed	Soon. Not for a long time.
5 Upright **5** Reversed	Continue and you will flourish. Not yet.
6 Upright **6** Reversed	In less time than you think. Very gradual change.
7 Upright **7** Reversed	This year. The hundredth day of the year.
8 Upright **8** Reversed	Yes. The fifteenth day of the month.
9 Upright **9** Reversed	There is some cause of delay. In two years' time.

Tablet of the Sun: meanings (continued)

Number and position of paper	Meaning
10 Upright	You are wrong to be impatient.
10 Reversed	Never.
11 Upright	Right away.
11 Reversed	In months rather than days.
12 Upright	Very soon.
12 Reversed	Three times.
13 Upright	Find your lucky day.
13 Reversed	Sooner than you imagine.
14 Upright	There is not much longer to wait.
14 Reversed	Leave well alone for as long as you can.
15 Upright	It seems to have no chance of happening.
15 Reversed	Highly improbable.
16 Upright	In one year's time.
16 Reversed	In a while.

Tablet of Jupiter

This tablet will answer questions concerned with doubts, worries, legal problems, and justice.

See next page for meanings.

Tablet of Jupiter: meanings

Number and position of paper	Meaning
1 Upright	You have been misjudged.
1 Reversed	Your judgment was hasty.
2 Upright	The truth will out.
2 Reversed	You will not play a major part.
3 Upright	Your judgment was much too hasty.
3 Reversed	You could not escape this trouble.
4 Upright	This cloud will pass.
4 Reversed	Things will soon improve.
5 Upright	You are in the wrong.
5 Reversed	Be brave, you have done no wrong.
6 Upright	You are most certainly right.
6 Reversed	This is an injustice.
7 Upright	Learn from your own experience.
7 Reversed	Take care.
8 Upright	You already know the truth.
8 Reversed	There is no danger.

Number and position of paper	Meaning
9 Upright	No one can answer the question for you.
9 Reversed	Justice will triumph in the end.
10 Upright	There will be little delay.
10 Reversed	Do not be afraid without reason.
11 Upright	Try once more.
11 Reversed	Speak out boldly.
12 Upright	Do not be afraid.
12 Reversed	No, which is a good thing.
13 Upright	Yes, and right will prevail.
13 Reversed	You are not in error.
14 Upright	Things are not as black as you think.
14 Reversed	Make your plans slowly and carefully.
15 Upright	It is a foolish scandal.
15 Reversed	Do not be anxious.
16 Upright	You were in the worng.
16 Reversed	Everything will come right in the end.

Tablet of Mars

This tablet will answer questions to do with work, business, or money.

8	13	6	2
3	5	4	16
10	7	9	16
14	1	15	11

See opposite for meanings.

Tablet of Mars: meanings

Number and position of paper	Meaning
1 Upright **1** Reversed	Money changes. Friends are more valuable than money.
2 Upright **2** Reversed	New work. It will be very expensive.
3 Upright **3** Reversed	It's up to you. There is a high risk.
4 Upright **4** Reversed	Happiness is preferable to wealth. Do not rely on it.
5 Upright **5** Reversed	The bad times will soon be over. There is the prospect of wealth.
6 Upright **6** Reversed	A big surprise. Be ready to take some blame.
7 Upright **7** Reversed	Think hard before giving your consent. Look at it from a different angle.
8 Upright **8** Reversed	Hard work is what is needed. Be less selfish and more considerate of others.

Tablet of Mars: meanings (continued)

Number and position of paper	Meaning
9 Upright	Prove that you can be trusted.
9 Reversed	If you persevere no-one can rob you of success.
10 Upright	Be very careful.
10 Reversed	Turn back.
11 Upright	Expect problems ahead.
11 Reversed	Take counsel of your second thoughts.
12 Upright	Your worries will soon be over.
12 Reversed	Exactly what you deserve.
13 Upright	Expect good luck.
13 Reversed	Money.
14 Upright	Be bold.
14 Reversed	It will be an improvement.
15 Upright	All's well.
15 Reversed	You will gain by an accident.
16 Upright	Have patience.
16 Reversed	Be brave.

Tablet of Mercury

This tablet will answer questions about journeys.

See next page for meanings.

Tablet of Mercury: meanings

Number and position of paper	Meaning
1 Upright **1** Reversed	In a while. Wants to be with you.
2 Upright **2** Reversed	Yes, it's all for the best. It's inadvisable.
3 Upright **3** Reversed	Better to stay where you are. You will decline.
4 Upright **4** Reversed	The prospect of a long journey. When you least expect it.
5 Upright **5** Reversed	Distant thoughts are turned to you. Some loss and some gain.
6 Upright **6** Reversed	A disappointment. It should not be long now.
7 Upright **7** Reversed	Not far. An enjoyable time.
8 Upright **8** Reversed	Yes, though it's not so very important. After careful thought.

Number and position of paper	Meaning
9 Upright	Modern transport has made the world shrink.
9 Reversed	Very doubtful indeed.
10 Upright	It will happen very suddenly.
10 Reversed	An unexpected route to happiness.
11 Upright	Definitely for the better.
11 Reversed	Westward.
12 Upright	Expect many changes.
12 Reversed	All will not be happiness.
13 Upright	Your hopes will be fulfilled.
13 Reversed	The distance is great.
14 Upright	Wait awhile.
14 Reversed	Soon.
15 Upright	All's for the best.
15 Reversed	The East beckons.
16 Upright	Don't go.
16 Reversed	Not yet.

TAROT

Definition Divination using a set of specially decorated cards.

History Some occultists claim that the origins of tarot lie with the priests of ancient Egypt, or ancient Babylon, or ancient Tibet. The exact origins of tarot are not clear, although its first recorded appearance was in medieval France, in about 1390. In medieval times people used the cards to play quite ordinary games, often for money, although practitioners today suggest that the tarot must be taken seriously. Some practitioners insist that the tarot is a repository for a special kind of lore, and the cards have always been associated with a slightly sinister mystery. Some refer to tarot as "the devil's picture book."

Modern methods The method of reading the tarot has changed little but requires considerable practice. Provided here is a description of the tarot cards and an explanation of how to use them for divination.

Equipment Although the European kind of tarot cards were more or less standardized in the eighteenth century, and their central figures remain the same, they have been constantly redesigned. As a consequence, sets of tarot cards can now be bought in a huge variety of styles, in shops specializing in the "occult," or via mail order through fortune-telling magazines. Some readers like to deal the cards onto a silk cloth.

Tarot cards
There are 78 cards in a tarot set, divided into two groups: the major arcana and the minor arcana.

The major arcana (sometimes known as the greater trumps) contains 22 cards representing stages in an individual's progress through life.

The minor arcana contains 56 cards and is divided into four suits: cups, swords, pentacles, and wands. Each suit contains 14 cards, numbered sequentially.

General guidelines
- Handle your own tarot cards as much as possible.
- Study your cards, think about them, and attune them to your own intuitive awareness.
- Do not use tarot cards frivolously.
- Practice using tarot cards until you become familiar with their symbolism.

THE MAJOR ARCANA
The 22 cards of the major arcana are all named, and begin with "The Fool" and end with "The World." Traditionally numbered, each is attributed with significant meaning. The first 11 cards represent the first half of life and tend to be outward-looking, oriented toward the world of positive action and development. The second 11 reflect a more meditative, quiet, inward-looking time that is focused on inward development. Because tarot cards are not double-headed they can be reversed when laid out. These meanings are included in the following summaries.

0 The Fool
Unnumbered, this card is often used as the significator, to represent the subject of the reading. Symbolizing new beginnings, potentiality, and fresh challenges, it is the most complex of the cards—"holy innocent," a wise man, and trickster, with all of humanity's contradictions (good/evil, angel/devil, male/female, etc.).
Reversed Beware of foolish lack of forethought.

1 Magician (or Jester)
A fortunate card indicating decisions to be made, progress in worldly understanding, and progress toward success. Only one step away from the Fool (as jester), it relates more to a stage magician—an entertainer—than to a master of magical lore.
Reversed Warns against an unwillingness to confront the real world, or against hesitation.

LA PAPESSE

L IMPERATRISE

2 High Priestess
Indicating a female
influence and the prospect
of light being shed on a
secret or problem, this card
suggests an element of
creativity, intuition, special
knowledge, the
nonrational, natural side of
wisdom and understanding
(including the psychic
sort).
Reversed Warns against
irrationality, insufficient
use of rational thought and
overemotionalism.

3 Empress
A fortunate card
suggesting a solid stability
and a natural growth and
creativity (perhaps a new
baby, material prosperity or
just general well-being). It
represents the fertility
principle, the caring,
loving, enriching, bountiful
symbol of the Earth
Mother.
Reversed Domestic
trouble and insecurity,
perhaps career setbacks or
sexual difficulties.

LEMPEREVR

LE PAPE

4 Emperor

For women, this card can mean achievement of ambition through forcefulness and controlled aggression, or a dominating male influence. For men, it is a fortunate card. A male symbol, the father figure to the Empress's mother, this card indicates energy, strength of will, success, authority, power, and the triumph of rationality.
Reversed Warns against weakness, submission.

5 High Priest

The male counterpart of the High Priestess, this card suggests spiritual rather than worldly power and authority; the gaining of understanding, not necessarily religious; intelligence, rational knowledge, inspiring perceptions, and wisdom. It can also refer to the influence of an important teacher or advisor.
Reversed Beware of misleading advice, lies.

6 Lovers

Relating to love relationships, this card involves choices made between attractions of the flesh and of the spirit. It suggests a rewarding relationship or a good marriage and indicates generally positive decisions.

Reversed A wrong choice will be made, perhaps involving sexual infidelity. Also warns of sexual difficulties.

7 Chariot

A card indicating progress, achievement, and travel and which represents an important stage in the advance through worldly life, with obstacles overcome and success gained through personal dynamism.

Reversed Beware of too much dynamism leading to ruthlessness.

8 Justice

This card suggests the person is to be judged—a positive sign, unless he or she is found wanting. A useful balance to the Chariot, this is a reminder of the need for balance and sound judgment, that a complete person needs more than material triumphs—that the heart and spirit must also be served.

Reversed Injustice, unfair or harsh judgment by others.

9 Hermit

A card indicating a need for inner growth and development, reevaluation, and perhaps counsel about the future. Like Justice, it shows the tarot moving away from outward advance toward less worldly and material considerations.

Reversed Warns against a refusal to think things out or to take notice; against imprudence and stubbornness.

LA ROVE DE FORTVNE

LA FORCE

10 Wheel of fortune
A fortunate card implying
destiny will work itself out
positively. A clear sign of a
new stage or beginning, it
alludes to the mystic idea
of karma, individual inner
growth toward wholeness
and harmony (symbolized
by the circular mandala);
that without change life
will stagnate, and luck will
play a part in decisions to
be made.
Reversed Ill luck, decline,
adversity, changes for the
worse.

11 Strength
Implies difficulties and
setbacks overcome by
inner resources. Indicates
the need to face
developments with
fortitude, courage and
moral fiber. Some experts
prefer to transpose the
positions of this card with
justice.
Reversed Obstacles will
not be overcome, owing to
lack of spiritual or moral
strength.

12 Hanged man

A card implying sacrifice or risk, perhaps a decision to abandon worldly values, to retreat into oneself, to seek the inner reality needed to become whole, from which will come enlightenment, and renewal.

Reversed When reversed, the man appears upright. Beware a rigid refusal to accept that there is more to life than the rational, practical world.

13 Death

A card which suggests that every setback or failure can bring new understanding, and therefore new hope. Inner, psychic and spiritual rebirth can only be achieved after true inner development requiring a kind of death of the worldly self.

Reversed Foreshadows destruction without renewal.

14 Temperance
A fortunate card for all enterprises demanding the balancing of many complex factors. It indicates the need for moderation and reminds us that a truly complete life exhibits a harmony between the material and spiritual.
Reversed Difficulty and setbacks caused by lack of harmony.

15 Devil
An ominous card suggesting what can happen if we let certain "inward" qualities—such as selfishness, the urge to wield power, sexual impulses—get out of balance or out of control. Controlled, the strength of such drives can be positive, an energy source for favorable development.
Reversed Warns against giving in to impulses, and the dark side of nature.

16 Tower

An unfortunate card suggesting the shattering of hopes and ambitions, of ruin and destruction. However, out of suffering can come understanding; out of destruction can come rebuilding.
Reversed Ruin and calamity needlessly brought upon oneself.

17 Star

A fortunate card of enlightenment and enhanced awareness, this indicates hope and renewal after calamity, and promises new and rich horizons, perhaps in previously unforeseen directions, once you have come through the bad times.
Reversed Warns against spiritual blindness that prevents seeing or taking advantage of new horizons.

18 Moon

An unfortunate card for the rational person, this indicates a time when only intuition, the nonrational side, can overcome obstacles. It suggests the nonrational must be used with care as it can lead toward a dangerous fantasy world.

Reversed Warns against fearing the nonrational and settling for a life of stagnation and sterility.

19 Sun

A card signifying a triumphant reward for coming through hardships. The goal is visible: it suggests illumination in every sense, adversity overcome, wholeness and harmony achieved.

Reversed Failure, the collapse of hopes, or at best, a superficial, dubious success.

LE IVGEMENT

LE MONDE

20 Judgment

This is a fortunate card signifying new beginnings. It concerns the day when you pause to weigh up what you have done and what you have become in your passage through life. It indicates the attainment of inner development, that your achieved goals are worthy, and you are now entering a time of serenity and happiness.
Reversed Regrets, recriminations, remorse.

21 World

The ultimate circular mandala, this card symbolizes triumph, fulfillment, and completion. The cycle of the major arcana begins again with the Fool, but perhaps with greater goals and on a higher plane.
Reversed A bleak immobility, the inability to progress on and up, ultimate failure rather than ultimate fulfillment.

THE MINOR ARCANA

The minor arcana contains 56 cards and is divided into four suits, each with its own sphere of influence. When cards in any of the four suits are dealt upside down, their meaning is reversed.

Spheres of influence

Suit	Spheres of influence
Cups	● Emotional matters ● Love ● Sex ● Marriage ● Fertility ● Creativity
Pentacles	● Wealth ● Finance ● Commerce ● Prosperity ● Economic security
Swords	● Activity ● Progress ● Opposition and conflict ● The need to impose order on chaos
Wands	● The mind ● The world of ideas ● Deep thought ● Intellectual strength ● Range ● Purposefulness

Suit of cups

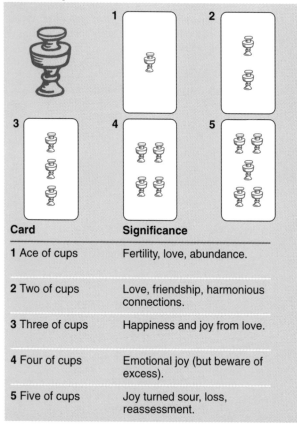

Card	Significance
1 Ace of cups	Fertility, love, abundance.
2 Two of cups	Love, friendship, harmonious connections.
3 Three of cups	Happiness and joy from love.
4 Four of cups	Emotional joy (but beware of excess).
5 Five of cups	Joy turned sour, loss, reassessment.

Card	Significance
6 Six of cups	Happy memories, the past reawakened.
7 Seven of cups	Ambition, hope (with forethought).
8 Eight of cups	Disappointment, search for new paths.
9 Nine of cups	Peace, contentment, fulfillment.
10 Ten of cups	Peace, happiness, achievement.

Suit of cups (continued)

Card	Significance
11 Knave of cups	A thoughtful, helpful youth.
12 Knight of cups	A fair, cheery youth, a lover.
13 Queen of cups	A bright, loving, creative woman.
14 King of cups	An intelligent, successful, worldly man.

Suit of swords

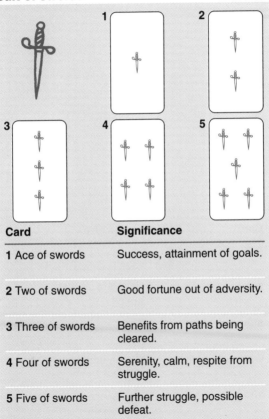

Card	Significance
1 Ace of swords	Success, attainment of goals.
2 Two of swords	Good fortune out of adversity.
3 Three of swords	Benefits from paths being cleared.
4 Four of swords	Serenity, calm, respite from struggle.
5 Five of swords	Further struggle, possible defeat.

Suit of swords (continued)

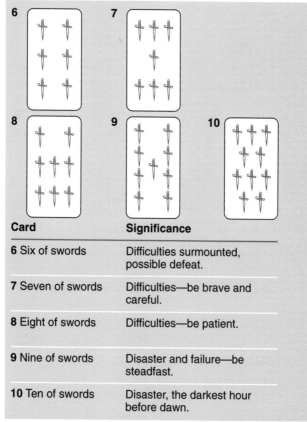

Card	Significance
6 Six of swords	Difficulties surmounted, possible defeat.
7 Seven of swords	Difficulties—be brave and careful.
8 Eight of swords	Difficulties—be patient.
9 Nine of swords	Disaster and failure—be steadfast.
10 Ten of swords	Disaster, the darkest hour before dawn.

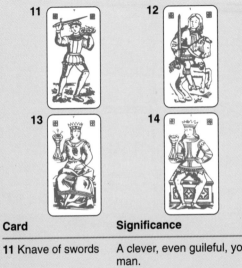

Card	Significance
11 Knave of swords	A clever, even guileful, young man.
12 Knight of swords	A soldier, a dark, strong youth.
13 Queen of swords	A dark, clever woman, a widow.
14 King of swords	A dark, authoritative man.

Suit of pentacles

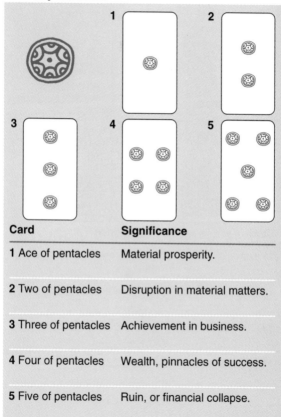

Card	Significance
1 Ace of pentacles	Material prosperity.
2 Two of pentacles	Disruption in material matters.
3 Three of pentacles	Achievement in business.
4 Four of pentacles	Wealth, pinnacles of success.
5 Five of pentacles	Ruin, or financial collapse.

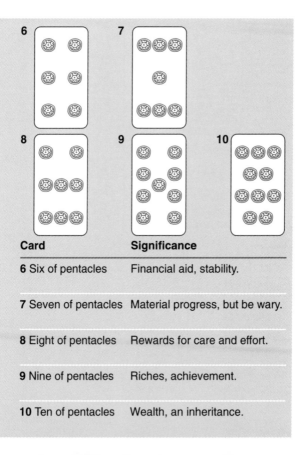

Card	Significance
6 Six of pentacles	Financial aid, stability.
7 Seven of pentacles	Material progress, but be wary.
8 Eight of pentacles	Rewards for care and effort.
9 Nine of pentacles	Riches, achievement.
10 Ten of pentacles	Wealth, an inheritance.

Suit of pentacles (continued)

Card	Significance
11 Knave of pentacles	A careful, sensible youth.
12 Knight of pentacles	A good, honorable young man.
13 Queen of spentacles	A sensible, generous, wealthy woman.
14 King of spentacles	A careful, practical, successful man.

Suit of wands

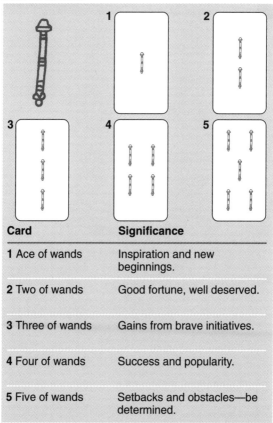

Card	Significance
1 Ace of wands	Inspiration and new beginnings.
2 Two of wands	Good fortune, well deserved.
3 Three of wands	Gains from brave initiatives.
4 Four of wands	Success and popularity.
5 Five of wands	Setbacks and obstacles—be determined.

Suit of wands (continued)

Card	Significance
6 Six of wands	Achievement, encouraging news.
7 Seven of wands	Troubles, but promising prospects.
8 Eight of wands	Forward progress—be confident.
9 Nine of wands	Opposition—be unyielding.
10 Ten of wands	Obstacles and struggles.

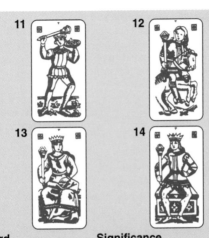

Card	Significance
11 Knave of wands	A dark, lively youth, an employee.
12 Knight of wands	A dark, energetic man, a journey.
13 Queen of wands	A practical, dominant woman.
14 King of wands	A powerful, determined man.

Choosing a significator

When using the minor arcana you may choose a significator—a card that represents the subject of the reading. Choose this from among the court cards, trying to ensure that it corresponds with your subject in terms of age, sex, complexion, and (where possible), personality.

Subject	For significator use:
WOMEN	
Fair-haired young woman	Queen of cups.
Fair-haired mature woman (especially if well-to-do)	Queen of pentacles.
Dark and perhaps dangerous woman	Queen of wands.
Dark and sad woman	Queen of swords.
MEN	
Fair young man, or any young man in love	Knight of cups.
Wealthy young man	Knight of pentacles.
Dark young man	Knight of wands.
Dangerous young man	Knave of wands.
Fair-haired mature man	King of cups.
Wealthy mature man	King of pentacles.
Mature man in a position of power	King of swords.
Dark and/or dangerous mature man	King of wands.

Reading the tarot

The reader and querant (the person whose fortune is to be told) should concentrate throughout the reading.

1 Place the deck in order, checking to ensure that every card is the right way up.
2 Choose the spread you are going to use.
3 Select the significator if one is needed for the spread you have chosen.
4 Shuffle the cards thoroughly, and in so doing, make sure that you turn some cards from top to bottom to ensure that some reversed cards will appear in the spread.
5 Hand the cards to the querant and ask him or her to repeat the shuffle.
6 Deal the cards, following any guidelines laid out in your chosen spread.

Horseshoe spread

This spread is useful for answering specific questions and is the most straightforward of the tarot spreads. You do not need a significator. Using the major arcana only, deal the first seven cards face up in the order shown.

Positions and their meanings
1 Past influences.
2 Present circumstances.
3 General future prospects.
4 Best course of action.
5 The attitudes of others.
6 Possible obstacles.
7 Final outcome.

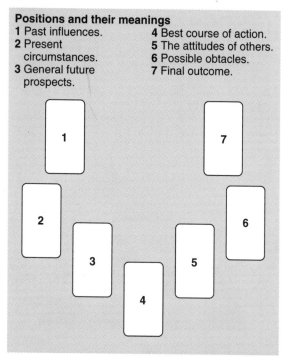

Seven-pointed star spread

This spread is useful for predicting events on the seven days after it is used. It can be used on any day of the week. Deal the first seven cards face down in the order shown. Place the significator face up in the center. Turn up the cards in order and interpret them.

Positions and their meanings

S Significator.	**4** Sunday.
1 Monday.	**5** Tuesday.
2 Wednesday.	**6** Thursday.
3 Friday.	**7** Saturday.

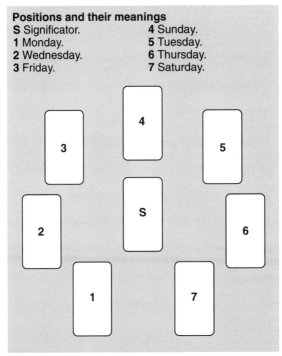

Celtic cross spread

Some readers believe this to be the most useful of the spreads as it can be used to answer general or specific questions, or to give a picture of the year ahead. You can use the whole tarot deck, or just the major arcana.

Card, phrase to be repeated, and meaning

1 "This covers you."
The querants present situation or state of mind.

2 "This crosses you."
Influences or events in the very near future.

3 "This crowns you."
The best course of action and the results of ignoring it.

4 "This is beneath you."
An event or matter in the past relevant to the present situation.

5 "This is behind you."
A more recent relevant event.

6 "This is before you."
The state of the querant's affairs in about six months' time.

7 "This is yourself."
Influences or events in the querant's main sphere of work.

8 "This is your house."
Influences or events in the querant's home or social life.

Choose a significator (**S**) and place it face up. Deal out the first 10 cards face down, in the order shown, and as you set them out repeat the phrases described below.

9 "Your hopes and fears."
Reflects the querant's feelings and influencing the likely outcome of events.

10 "This is what will come."
The final outcome: the accumulative statement of the whole spread.

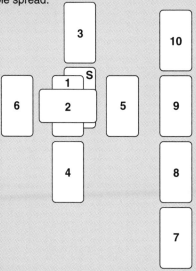

21 card spread

This is an in-depth yet easily interpreted tarot spread.
By giving each aspect of the reading three cards, more
information can be gathered than in, say, the horseshoe
spread, where just one card is used. Deal 21 cards face
down in the order shown. Place the significator face up
to the right. Turn over the cards and interpret them in
columns of three.

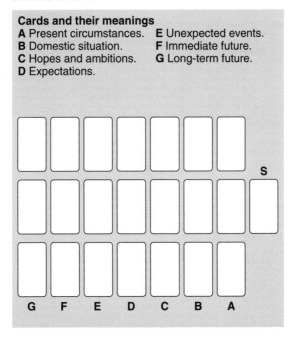

Cards and their meanings

A Present circumstances.   **E** Unexpected events.
B Domestic situation.   **F** Immediate future.
C Hopes and ambitions.   **G** Long-term future.
D Expectations.

S

G   F   E   D   C   B   A

Circular spread

Use this spread to give a general impression of the next 12 months, starting from the time of the reading. You do not need a significator. Deal the first 13 cards face down in the order shown. Interpret the thirteenth card first.

Positions and their meanings
- The first card refers to the coming month, the second to the month after that, and so on.
- The thirteenth card provides the main emphasis of the reading.

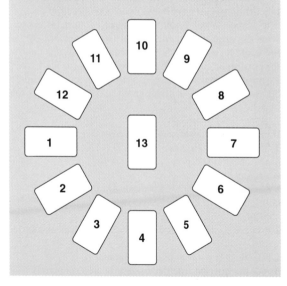

TASSEOGRAPHY

Definition Interpreting the shapes made by used tea leaves and using them to foretell the future.

History Tasseography probably began with the Chinese who were used to taking omens from the inside of bells. Their handleless teacups, when inverted, looked like small bells, and teacups became associated with the bell omens. Other residues have also been used—the Romans, for example, read the lees of their wine.

Modern methods The sediment left at the bottom of any drinking cup has always been considered of great importance in predicting the drinker's future, no matter what the original contents. Almost anything can therefore be used, and some people prefer to use the dregs of their coffee, interpreting them as for tea leaves.

Equipment For true tasseography you need a teacup and some tea made with loose tea leaves (do not use tea bags).

Preparing to make a reading

1 Use a teacup that has:
- a wide mouth
- sloping sides
- an inner surface that is smooth and undecorated.
- an inner surface that is either white or plain pastel color.

2 Prepare some tea that has fairly large leaves and little dust.

3 Fill the cup without using a strainer.

4 Ask the querant (the person whose fortune is to be

told) to drink the tea, leaving just enough liquid for the remaining leaves to be swilled.

5 Ask the querant to take the handle of the cup in the left hand and swill the leaves clockwise, three times, trying to ensure that the liquid remaining in the cup reaches right up to the brim.

6 Ask the querant to invert the cup onto a saucer and to let the liquid drain away for a count of seven.

7 Turn the cup the right way up and, holding it with the handle facing you, begin your reading, using the charts provided to help with your interpretation.

Hints for making a reading

- Practice frequently. It is not uncommon to find tasseography difficult at first, and many people find they have trouble identifying the different shapes and symbols in the leaves. Practice and experience will soon increase your levels of perception.

- Relax. One way to improve your abilities is to let your mind range freely, and allow your instincts and imagination to take over.

- Take a whole view. As with other forms of fortune telling, it is important that you consider the overall picture and do not just rely on individual sections of the reading. Do not consider symbols in isolation, but in relation to one another. Take into account their predominance, clarity, positions, sizes and proportions.

- Consider the overall appearance of the cup. A small scattering of just a few leaves implies a tidy, disciplined mind, whereas a great many leaves suggests a rich, full life.

Reading the position of leaves in the cup
The handle of the cup represents the querant (**a**) and
symbols are read in relation to the handle.

Position of symbol	Meaning
Close to the handle (**a**)	Something occurring close to the querant's home.
Pointing toward the handle (**b**)	Something approaching.
Pointing away from the handle (**c**)	Something departing.
Near the rim of the cup (**d**)	Events occurring in the present or near future.
Near the bottom of the cup (**e**)	Events occurring in the more distant future.
At the bottom of the cup (**f**)	Indicates ill fortune.

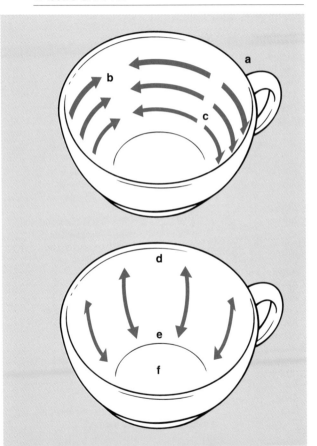

Tea leaf symbols

Symbol	Meaning
Abbey	Freedom from worry.
Ace of clubs	A letter.
Ace of diamonds	A present.
Ace of hearts	Happiness.
Ace of spades	Large building.
Acorn	Success. At top of cup—financial success; near middle of cup—good health; near bottom of cup—improvement in health or finances.
Aircraft	Sudden journey, not without risk. Can imply disappointment. If broken—an accident.
Alligator	Treachery, an accident.
Anchor	At top of cup—success in business and romance; middle of cup—prosperous voyage; bottom of cup—social success; obscured—anticipate difficulties.
Angel	Good news.
Ankle	Instability.
Ant	Success through perseverance.
Anvil	Conscientious effort.
Apple	Business achievement.
Apron	A new friend.
Arc	Ill health, accidents.
Arch	Journey abroad, a wedding.
Arrow	Bad news.
Ax	Difficulties.
Baby	Series of small worries.
Bag	A trap ahead. If open—you can escape; if closed—you will be trapped.

Symbol	Meaning
Bagpipes	Disappointment.
Ball	A person connected with sport, or variable fortunes in your life.
Balloon	Short-term troubles.
Barrel	A party.
Basin	Trouble at home. If broken—serious trouble.
Basket	If empty—money worries; if full—a present; near handle of cup—a baby; near top of cup—possessions; full of flowers—social success; surrounded by dots—unexpected money coming.
Bat	False friends, a journey ending in disappointment.
Bath	Disappointment.
Bayonet	A minor accident, a spiteful remark.
Beans	Poverty.
Bear	Facing handle—irrational decisions cause difficulties; facing away from handle—a journey.
Bed	Inertia.
Bee	Social success, good news. Near handle of cup—friends gathering; swarm of bees—success with an audience.
Beehive	Prosperity.
Beetle	Scandal, difficult undertaking.
Bell	Unexpected news. Near top of cup—promotion; near bottom of cup—sad news; two bells—joy; several bells—a wedding.

(continued)

Tea leaf symbols (continued)

Symbol	Meaning
Bellows	Plans will meet with setbacks.
Bird	Good news.
Birdcage	Obstacles, quarrels.
Bird's nest	Domestic harmony, love.
Bishop	Good luck coming.
Boat	Visit from a friend, a safe refuge.
Book	Open—expect legal actions, future success; closed—delay, difficult studies.
Boomerang	Treachery, envy.
Boot	Achievement, protection from pain. Pointing away from handle—dismissal; broken—failure.
Bottle	One bottle—pleasure; several bottles—illness.
Bouquet	Love and happiness.
Bow, bow and arrow	Scandal, gossip.
Box	Open—romantic troubles solved; closed—the lost will be found.
Bracelet	Impending marriage.
Branch	With leaves—a birth; without leaves—a disappointment.
Bread	Avoid waste.
Bridge	An opportunity for success.
Broom	Small worries disappear, a false friend.
Buckle	Disappointments ahead.
Bugle	Hard work necessary.
Building	A move.
Bull	Quarrels, enmity.
Buoy	Keep hoping.

Symbol	Meaning
Bush	New friends, fresh opportunities.
Butterfly	Frivolity, fickleness. Surrounded by dots—frittering away money.
Cab	A disappointment.
Cabbage	Jealousy causes complications at work.
Cage	A proposal.
Camel	Useful news.
Candle	Help from others, pursuit of knowledge.
Cannon	News of a soldier or a government employee.
Cap	Trouble ahead—be careful.
Car	Good fortune.
Cart	Success in business.
Castle	Financial gain through marriage, a strong character rising to prominence.
Cat	A quarrel, treachery, a false friend.
Cattle	Prosperity.
Chain	An engagement or wedding.
Chair	An unexpected guest. Surrounded by dots—financial improvements.
Cherries	A happy love affair.
Chessmen	Difficulties ahead.
Chimney	Hidden risks.
Church	Ceremony, unexpected money.
Cigar	New friends.
Circle	Success, a wedding. With a dot—a baby; with small lines nearby—efforts hampered.
Claw	A hidden enemy.

(continued)

Tea leaf symbols (continued)

Symbol	Meaning
Clock	Avoid delay, think of the future, a recovery from illness.
Clouds	Trouble ahead. Surrounded by dots—money troubles ahead.
Clover	Prosperity.
Coat	A parting, end of a friendship.
Cockatoo	Trouble among friends.
Coffeepot	Slight illness.
Coffin	Bad news.
Coin	Repayment of debts.
Collar	Dependence on others for success and happiness.
Column	Promotion, success, arrogance.
Comb	Deceit, a false friend.
Comet	An unexpected visitor.
Compass	Travel, a change of job.
Corkscrew	Curiosity causing trouble.
Crab	An enemy.
Crescent	A journey.
Cross	A sacrifice, trouble, ill health. Within a square—trouble averted; two crosses—long life; three crosses—great achievement.
Crown	Honor, success, a wish coming true, a legacy.
Crutches	Help from a friend.
Cup	Reward for effort.
Curtain	A secret.
Cymbal	Insincere love.
Daffodil	Great happiness.

Symbol	Meaning
Dagger	Impetuousness, danger ahead, enemies plotting.
Daisy	Happiness in love.
Dancer	Disappointment.
Deer	A dispute or quarrel.
Desk	Letter containing good news.
Devil	Evil influences.
Dish	Quarrel at home.
Dog	Good friends. If running—good news, happy meetings; at bottom of cup—friend in trouble.
Donkey	Be patient and optimistic.
Door	Strange occurrence.
Dot	This emphasizes the importance of the nearest symbol. Several dots—money.
Dove	Good fortune.
Dragon	Unforeseen changes, trouble.
Drum	Scandal, gossip, a new job, arguments.
Duck	Money coming in.
Dustpan	Strange news about a friend.
Eagle	A change for the better.
Ear	Unexpected news.
Earrings	Misunderstanding.
Easel	Artistic success.
Egg	Prosperity, success—the more eggs the better.
Eggcup	Danger is passing.
Elephant	Wisdom, strength, lasting success, a trustworthy friend.
Engine	News on its way fast.

(continued)

Tea leaf symbols (continued)

Symbol	Meaning
Envelope	Good news.
Eye	Overcoming difficulties, take care.
Face	One face—a change, a setback; several faces—a party.
Fairy	Joy and enchantment.
Fan	Flirtation, indiscretion.
Feather	Instability, inconsistency, lack of concentration.
Feet	An important decision.
Fence	Limitation to activities, minor setbacks, future success.
Fender	Beware of a person you dislike.
Fern	Disloyalty, an unfaithful lover.
Finger	Emphasizes the symbol at which it points.
Fir	Artistic success. The higher the tree, the better.
Fire	Achievement, avoid overhasty reactions.
Fireplace	Matters related to your home.
Fish	Good fortune in all things, health, wealth, and happiness.
Fist	An argument.
Flag	Danger ahead.
Flower	Wish coming true.
Fly	Domestic irritations. The more flies, the more petty problems.
Font	A birth.
Fork	A false friend, flattery.
Forked line	Decisions to be made.
Fountain	Future success and happiness.

Symbol	Meaning
Fox	A deceitful friend.
Frog	Success through a change of home or job, avoid self-importance.
Fruit	Prosperity.
Gallows	Social failure, enemies confounded.
Garden roller	Difficulties ahead.
Garland	Success, great honor.
Gate	Opportunity, future happiness.
Geese	Invitations, unexpected visitors.
Giraffe	Think before you speak.
Glass	Integrity.
Glove	A challenge.
Goat	Enemies threaten, news from a sailor.
Gondola	Romance, travel.
Gramophone	Pleasure.
Grapes	Happiness.
Grasshopper	News of a much-traveled friend.
Greyhound	Good fortune.
Guitar	Happiness in love.
Gun	Trouble, quarrels.
Hammer	Overcoming obstacles, ruthlesness, work that is uncongenial.
Hand	Friendship.
Handcuffs	Trouble ahead.
Hare	Timidity, news of a friend.
Harp	Harmony in love.
Hat	A new occupation, a change. Bent and broken—failure likely; in bottom of cup— a rival; on side of cup—diplomacy.
Hawk	Sudden danger, jealousy.

(continued)

Tea leaf symbols (continued)

Symbol	Meaning
Hayrick	Think before you act.
Head	New opportunities.
Heart	Love and marriage, a trustworthy friend.
Heather	Good fortune.
Hen	Domestic bliss.
Hill	Obstacles, setbacks.
Hoe	Hard work leading to success.
Holly	An important occurrence in the winter.
Horn	Abundance.
Horse	Galloping—good news from a lover; head only—romance.
Horseshoe	Good luck.
Hourglass	A decision that must be made.
House	Security.
Iceberg	Danger.
Initials	Usually those of people known to you. If next to a triangle, the initials of strangers.
Inkpot	A letter.
Insect	Minor problems soon overcome.
Ivy leaf	Reliable friend.
Jester	Party or social gathering. Alternatively—avoid frivolity, be serious.
Jewelry	A present.
Jockey	Speculation.
Jug	Gaining in importance, good health.
Kangaroo	Domestic harmony.
Kettle	Minor illness. Near handle of cup—domestic bliss; near or at bottom of cup—domestic strife.

Symbol	Meaning
Key	New opportunities, doors opening. Crossed keys—success; two keys near bottom of cup—robbery.
Keyhole	Beware of idle curiosity.
King	A powerful ally.
Kite	Wishes coming true, do not take chances, scandal.
Knife	Broken relationships. Near handle of cup—divorce; on bottom of cup—lawsuits; crossed knives—arguments.
Ladder	Promotion.
Lamp	Near handle of cup—money; near rim of cup—celebration; on side of cup—personal loss; on bottom of cup—postponed spcial event; two lamps—two marriages.
Leaf	Prosperity, good fortune.
Leopard	News of a journey.
Letter	News. Near dots—news about money.
Lighthouse	Trouble threatening, but averted. Success through a friend.
Lines	Straight and clear—progress, journeys; wavy—uncertainty, disappointment; slanting—business failure.
Lion	Influential friends.
Lock	Obstacles in your path.
Loop	Impulsive actions could bring trouble.
Mask	Deception.
Medal	A reward.

(continued)

Tea leaf symbols (continued)

Symbol	Meaning
Mermaid	Temptation, an offer that is not what it seems.
Miter	Honors.
Monkey	A flattering mischief-maker.
Monster	Terror.
Monument	Lasting happiness.
Moon	Full—a love affair; first quarter—new projects; last quarter—fortune declining; obscured—depression; surrounded by dots—marriage for money.
Mountain	Obstacle, high ambition.
Mouse	Theft.
Mushroom	Growth, setbacks. Near handle of cup—a home in the country.
Music	Good fortune.
Nail	Malice, injustice, sharp pain.
Necklace	Complete—admirers; broken—the end of a relationship.
Needle	Admiration.
Net	Traps for the unwary.
Numbers	Indicate a timescale, the number of days before an event occurs.
Nun	Quarantine.
Nurse	Illness.
Nutcrackers	Difficulty is passing.
Oak	Good fortune.
Oar	A small worry, help in difficulties.
Octopus	Danger.
Opera glasses	A quarrel, loss of a friend.
Ostrich	Travel.

Symbol	Meaning
Owl	Gossip, scandal, failure. At bottom of cup—financial failure; near handle—domestic failure.
Oyster	Courtship.
Padlock	Open—a surprise; closed—a warning.
Palm tree	Success, honor, happiness in love.
Parachute	Escape from danger.
Parasol	A new lover.
Parcel	A surprise.
Parrot	A scandal, a journey.
Peacock	With tail spread—riches, land; surrounded by dots—a life of luxury; next to a ring—a rich marriage.
Pear	Comfort, financial ease.
Pentagon	Intellectual balance.
Pepperpot	A troublesome secret.
Pig	Material success begins emotional problems.
Pigeon	Sitting—an improvement in trade; flying—important news.
Pillar	Supportive friends.
Pipe	Thoughts, soultion to a problem, keep an open mind.
Pistol	Danger.
Pitchfork	Quarrels.
Policeman	Secret enemy.
Pot	Service to society.
Profile	New friend.
Pump	Generosity.
Purse	Profit. At bottom of cup—loss.

(continued)

Tea leaf symbols (continued)

Symbol	Meaning
Pyramid	Solid success.
Question mark	Hesitancy, caution.
Rabbit	Timidity, be brave.
Railway	Long journey.
Rainbow	Happiness, prosperity.
Rake	Be organized.
Rat	Treachery.
Raven	Bad news.
Razor	Quarrels, partings.
Reptiles	Treacherous friend.
Rider	Hasty news.
Ring	Completion. Near top of cup—marriage; near middle of cup—proposal; near bottom of cup—long engagement; complete ring—happy marriage; broken ring, or ring with a cross next to it—broken engagement; two rings—plans working out.
Rocks	Difficulties.
Rose	Popularity.
Saucepan	Anxieties.
Saw	Interfering outsider.
Scales	A lawsuit. Balanced scales—justice; unbalanced scales—injustice.
Scepter	Power, authority.
Scissors	Domestic arguments, separation.
Scythe	Danger.
Shamrock	Good luck, wish coming true.
Sheep	Good fortune.
Shell	Good news.

Symbol	Meaning
Ship	Successful journey.
Shoe	A change for the better.
Sickle	Disappointment in love.
Signpost	Draws attention to the symbol at which it points.
Skeleton	Loss of money, ill health.
Snake	Hatred, an enemy.
Spade	Hard work leads to success, or avoid taking sides.
Spider	Determined and persistent, secretive, money coming.
Spoon	Generosity.
Square	A symbol of protection, comfort, peace. Alternatively—restrictions, setbacks.
Squirrel	Prosperity after a hard time.
Star	Good health, happiness. Five-pointed star—good fortune; eight-pointed star—accidents, reverses; five stars together—success without happiness; seven stars together—grief.
Steeple	Slight delay, bad luck.
Steps	An improvement in life.
Sun	Happiness, success, power.
Swallow	Decisiveness, unexpected journeys.
Swan	Smooth progress, contented life.
Sword	Disappointments, quarrels.
Table	Social gathering. Surrounded by dots—financial conference.
Teapot	Committee meeting.
Telephone	Forgetfulness causes trouble.

(continued)

Tea leaf symbols (continued)

Symbol	Meaning
Telescope	Adventure.
Tent	Travel.
Thimble	Domestic changes.
Toad	Beware of flattery.
Torch	A turn for the better.
Tortoise	Criticism.
Tower	Opportunity, disappointment.
Tree	Changes for the better, ambitions fulfilled. Surrounded by dots—your fortune lies in the country.
Triangle	Something unexpected. Point upward—brings success; point downward—brings failure.
Trident	Success at sea.
Trunk	A long journey, fateful decisions.
Umbrella	Annoyances, a need for shelter. If open—shelter found; if shut—shelter refused.
Unicorn	A secret wedding.
Urn	Wealth, happiness.
Vase	A friend in need.
Vegetables	Unhappiness followed by contentment.
Violin	Egotism.
Volcano	Emotions out of control.
Vulture	Loss, theft, an enemy in authority.
Wagon	A wedding.
Walking stick	A visitor.
Wasp	Trouble in love.
Waterfall	Prosperity.
Weather vane	A difficulty, indecisiveness.
Whale	Business success.

Symbol	Meaning
Wheel	Complete—good fortune, earned success; broken—disappointment; near rim of cup—unexpected money.
Wheelbarrow	A meeting with an old friend.
Windmill	Business success through hard work rather than brilliance.
Window	Open—good luck through a friend; closed—disappointment through a friend.
Wings	Messages.
Wishbone	A wish granted.
Wolf	Jealousy, selfishness.
Woman	Pleasure.
Worms	Scandal.
Wreath	Happiness ahead.
Yacht	Pleasure.
Yoke	Being dominated.
Zebra	Adventures overseas, an unsettled life.

READING COFFEE GROUNDS

Coffee grounds can be prepared in much the same way as tea leaves and are read similarly.

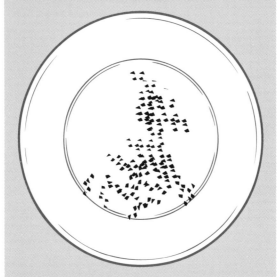

1 Make a cup of coffee and give it to the person whose fortune is being told.

2 Ask that person to drink the coffee but to leave enough liquid in the cup to swill the grounds. Swirl the cup and invert it onto a saucer. Alternatively, swirl the grounds over a clean white plate so that there is a scattering of symbols across the plate.

3 Interpret the symbols as you would for tea leaves.

MOLYBDOMANCY

This is a method of forming images, similar to tasseography, but which does not use tea leaves. It was practiced as a by-product of alchemists' attempts to translate base metals into gold. In medieval times, molten tin or lead was dipped into water to form characteristic shapes. The shapes were then interpreted in a manner similar to tasseography.

Lead

Tin

CEROMACY

Ceromancy is divination using wax. It was popular in the eighteenth century when it was common to use wax in sealing correspondence. Melted wax was allowed to drip into a shallow dish of cold water and the resulting shapes were interpreted. Ceromancy is still practiced by Voodoo priests, who conduct ceromantic readings that can last from dusk till dawn.

UNDERSTANDING ASTROLOGY

Definition Divination using the eight planets in our solar system, the Sun, the Moon, and the twelve constellations of stars beyond our solar system (collectively referred to as the zodiac). Astrology—understanding the significance of stars—is related to, but different from, astronomy—study of the movements and positions of the stars.

History People had begun to look at the stars for guidance as long ago as 8000 B.C. Astrologers were

Important conventions used in astrology

- The Earth is seen to be at the center of the universe.
- The Sun and Moon are referred to as planets. There are therefore *ten* astrological planets that appear to move around the Earth.
- Each of the ten planets is thought to influence the lives of people on Earth.
- How the planets influence us is determined by the signs of the zodiac, of which there are twelve, each based on a constellation of stars.
- In order to assess character and determine future events, astrologers construct horoscopes or birth charts, symbolic maps of the sky that reflect the time and place on Earth that a person was born.
- Symbols are commonly used to represent the planets and signs of the zodiac. These are illustrated in a separate chart.

employed by the Assyrians, Babylonians, Egyptians, and Mayans to observe, record, and predict the positions of stars and events which were believed to be important for their survival and prosperity. The mathematician Ptolemy wrote the first known textbook on astrology while he was working in Egypt between A.D. 150 and 180. The Greeks furthered the spread of astrology, introducing it to India and, later, to the Arab world. The word planet comes from the Greek *planetes*, meaning wanderer; the word horoscope comes from two Greek words, *horos* meaning time, and *skopos* meaning observer.

Astrology was considered synonymous with astronomy until the seventeenth century; then, during the eighteenth and nineteenth centuries, research into this area of divination declined. Twentieth-century research sometimes supports astrological theories and sometimes condemns them. There is, however, continued interest in this method of divination.

Modern methods Modern birth charts are similar to the charts used by the Greeks during the first and second centuries A.D. Today, however, astrology is used more to assess character and potential than to predict future events. Analytical psychology is used in addition to ancient mythology for the interpretation of charts.

Equipment Information provided here will enable you to understand different aspects of the birth chart. Birth charts themselves are best constructed by professional astrologers, as they require the use of detailed and often very complex astronomical data.

ASTROLOGICAL SYMBOLS

Astrologists use symbols (sometimes referred to as
glyphs) to represent the ten planets and the 12 signs of
the zodiac.

Planetary symbols

Planet	Symbol	Planet	Symbol
Sun	☉	Jupiter	♃
Moon	☽	Saturn	♄
Mercury	☿	Uranus	♅
Venus	♀	Neptune	♆
Mars	♂	Pluto	♇

Zodiac signs

Constellation	Zodiac sign	Constellation	Zodiac sign
Aries	♈	Libra	♎
Taurus	♉	Scorpio	♏
Gemini	♊	Sagittarius	♐
Cancer	♋	Capricorn	♑
Leo	♌	Aquarius	♒
Virgo	♍	Pisces	♓

PARTS OF THE BIRTH CHART

A birth chart (example, *right*) consists of a circle
(representing the Earth) (**a**) surrounded by another,
larger circle, that is divided into 12 sections (called
"houses") (**b**). The relative positions of the planets (**c**)
are written inside the house segments (using symbols)
and the signs of the zodiac (**d**) appear around the edge
of the birth chart (also as symbols), always in the same
order. A horizontal line runs across the chart and is
called a cusp (**e**). This cusp is always in the ascendant
position (ASC), the position of the Sun as it rose on the
eastern horizon on the date of birth. The cusp of a sign
or house marks its starting point. On this chart, Virgo is
the ascending (or rising) sign and determines the
placing of the wheel against the signs of the zodiac.
Another cusp is included that indicates the position of
the Sun at noon on the date of birth (**f**). It is represented
by the letters MC, standing for the Latin, *medium coeli*,
meaning midheaven. South is always placed at the top
of the chart. This means that the Sun sign of a person
born during the night will be in the lower half of the
chart; the Sun sign for a person born during the day will
be in the upper half of the chart. If the time of birth is
not known, the Sun is placed in the midheaven position
and the houses omitted. Note that the cusps for the first,
fourth, seventh, and tenth houses are particularly
important and are indicated by double lines.

A sample birth chart

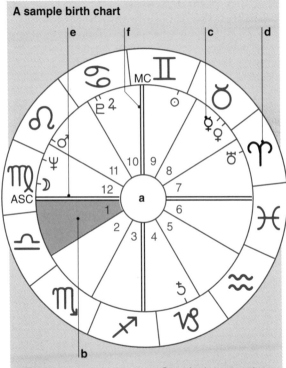

a Earth
b A "house"
c A planet
d Zodiac sign

e Cusp in the ascendant
  position
f Cusp indicating
  midheaven

FINDING YOUR SUN SIGN

You can find your Sun sign by using the chart on the next few pages, providing you have your date of birth. Note, however, that the Sun enters and leaves signs on

Date of birth	Sun sign	Symbol
March 22–April 20	Aries	♈
April 21–May 21	Taurus	♉
May 22–June 22	Gemini	♊
June 23–July 23	Cancer	♋
July 24–August 23	Leo	♌
August 24–Sept 23	Virgo	♍

slightly different dates in some years. So if you are born on or near a cusp of a sign, you will need to check a more detailed table of Sun sign changes.

Date of birth	Sun sign	Symbol
Sept 24–Oct 23	Libra	♎
Oct 24–Nov 22	Scorpio	♏
Nov 23–Dec 22	Sagittarius	♐
Dec 23–Jan 19	Capricorn	♑
Jan 20–Feb 19	Aquarius	♒
Feb 20–March 21	Pisces	♓

SHAPE OF THE BIRTH CHART

Before considering individual aspects of the birth chart
in detail, it is useful to take an overall view of the chart
in order to help form a general impression of a person's
personality. Look at a chart and examine the shape
made by the arrangement of planets. (It does not matter
what the individual planets are, just where they are
located on the chart.) There are seven major
arrangements of planets, and therefore seven birth chart
"shapes": bucket, locomotive, splash, seesaw, bundle,
splay and bowl. Each shape is thought to coincide with
a different personality type, all seven of which are
shown here—dots representing the planets—with
aspects of the corresponding personality represented
too.

Bucket

Nine of the planets fall in one
half of the chart; the tenth
planet (called the singleton) is
opposite them, and forms the
handle of the bucket.

Aspects of the bucket personality
- Energies are directed toward the achievement of
  one objective. (The singleton often indicates the
  nature of this purpose.)
- Bucket personalities may have low concern for
  self-preservation.

Locomotive

Planets are arranged fairly evenly around nine consecutive zodiac signs. There is an empty group of three signs.

Aspects of the locomotive personality

- Exceptional drive and application to the task in hand.
- The leading planet moving clockwise around the wheel may indicate which area of the personality is the prime motivating force.

Splash

Planets occupy as many zodiac signs as possible and may be spread fairly evenly around the wheel.

Aspects of the splash personality

- Splash personalities have wide interests.
- One of the negative aspects of these people is that they may spread themselves too thinly.

Seesaw

Two groups of planets appear opposite each other, ideally with five planets in each group (although the number of planets may vary); there are two or more empty signs in the two empty sections.

Aspects of the seesaw personality
- These people see both sides of an issue, and may view life from two points of view.
- People with a seesaw chart may need to balance their activities and interests.

Bundle

The rarest of the chart shapes. Planets are grouped closely together in four or five consecutive signs.

Aspects of the bundle personality
- A personality with a driving specialist interest.

Splay

There must be at least one group of two or three planets placed closely together while the rest are distributed around the chart. Empty signs are usually distributed evenly as well.

Aspects of the splay personality
● People with splay charts are individualists who do not like being regimented or classified.

Bowl

All planets fall into approximately half of the chart. Further information about bowl charts is provided on the next few pages.

Aspects of the bowl personality
● People with bowl charts are very self-contained.
● They scoop up experiences.
● The leading planet of the bowl may lead them to various experiences.

Bowl shape charts

In a bowl chart all of the planets fall in approximately half of the chart. There are four different types of bowl charts, named according to the semicircle of the chart in which the planets fall. Each provides yet further

Night bowl

In this type of chart planets fall within the lower half of the bowl.

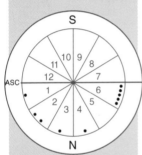

Day bowl

In this type of chart planets fall within the upper half of the bowl.

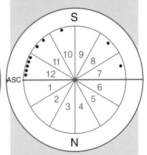

Personality aspects
- A natural loner.
- Shy.
- May have unusual insights.
- May have a natural artistic talent.

Personality aspects
- Ambitious.
- Calculating.
- Self-centered.
- Has many acquaintances.
- Has a small number of very close friends.

information about a bowl chart person's personality. Use the examples here to see what type of bowl chart you have. Remember that in birth charts, south is always placed at the *top* of the chart.

West bowl
All the planets are situated in the right semicircle of the bowl.

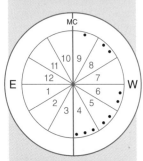

East bowl
All the planets are situated in the left semicircle of the bowl.

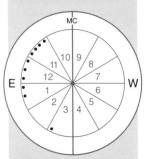

Personality aspects
- Ability to develop good human relations.
- Socially diplomatic.
- Strongly influenced by the opinions of others.
- Finds self-assertion difficult.

Personality aspects
- Individualistic.
- Dislikes taking orders.
- Dislikes compromise.
- May have difficulty with personal relationships.

Semicircles and quarters

Special lines are used to divide up birth charts into semicircles and quarters, each of which represents a different aspect of the personality.

The horizon or equator, night and day planets

The line extending across the middle of the chart (**a**) is called the horizon or equator. Planets below this line—placed in houses 1–6—are in the northern half (**b**) of the chart and are called the night planets. They represent privacy and subjectivity. Planets above this line—placed in houses 7–12—are in the southern half (**c**) of the chart and are called the day planets. They represent an outgoing nature and objectivity.

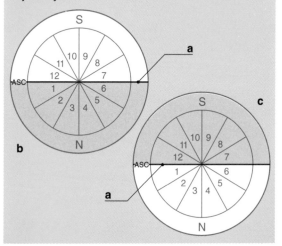

The meridian, east and western planets
The line extending down the middle of the chart is
called the meridian (**a**). Planets to the left of the
meridian are called eastern planets (**b**) and
represent free will and independence. Planets to the
right of the meridian are called western planets (**c**)
and represent flexibility and dependence.

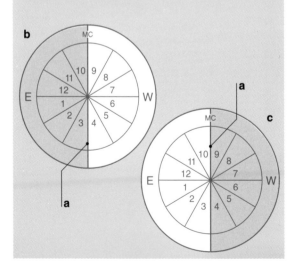

The four quarters

Combining night and day semicircles with the east and west semicircles determines four quarters.

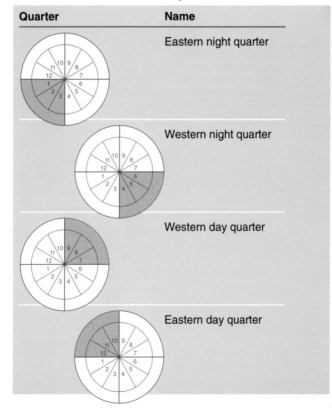

Quarter	Name
	Eastern night quarter
	Western night quarter
	Western day quarter
	Eastern day quarter

Each quarter represents a different aspect of the personality, and each contains three houses.

Houses	Characteristics
1,2,3	• Love of privacy • Dislike of compromise
4,5,6	• Imagination • A reserved nature
7,8,9	• Ambition • Indecisiveness
10,11,12	• Rebellious independence

OVERVIEW OF THE PLANETS

One of the components essential to a birth chart reading
is the significance and influence of the planets. These
are usually listed in a traditional order of importance,
starting with the Sun, and are considered as they appear
in the different zodiac signs and houses.

Planets reflecting the life cycle

A person's essential nature is symbolized by the
positions of the Sun, Moon, and ascendant, each of
which is related to a different aspect of a person's life
cycle. The ascendant represents the future outlook, the
Moon reflects moods to which we have become
conditioned in the past, and the Sun represents
personality in the present. It is said that the Sun and
Moon dominate the chart during the earlier part of life,
as the Sun attempts to express itself and come to terms
with the Moon's influence. The ascendant symbolizes
the outlook of a person and influences physical
appearance. It is important because it is the leader of
the succession of signs and houses around the chart. It
shares the same potentials as the Sun, and so the same
interpretations apply. It may be in any one of the zodiac
signs but is always on the cusp of the first house.

Personal planets

The Sun, Moon, Mercury, Venus, and Mars move
quickly through the signs. The Moon remains in a sign
for only about two days; Mars may stay in a sign for
two months. These planets symbolize individual
resources and are regarded as personal planets.

Generation planets

These are Uranus, Neptune, and Pluto. They represent collective resources and move very slowly. Uranus takes about seven years to move through a sign; Neptune takes about 14 years; Pluto takes 13–32 years. They show how people are likely to respond to larger social issues.

Planets: areas of influence

By locating the position of a planet on the birth chart it is possible to answer "what?" questions. For example, each planet has an area of influence (indicated by the chart below). In order to determine what moods a person might experience, it is necessary to find the location of the Moon; in order to determine what responsibilities are likely, Saturn must be located; to find out what changes are likely, find Uranus, etc.

Planet	Symbolism	Area of influence
Sun	Source of life	Personality
Moon	Mirror of life	Moods
Mercury	Messenger	Thoughts
Venus	Goddess of love	Feelings and values
Mars	Warrior	Action and drive
Jupiter	Prophet	Expansion
Saturn	Lawgiver	Responsibilities
Uranus	Awakener	Changes
Neptune	Mystic	Imagination
Pluto	Dark Lord	Transformation

THE SUN: source of life

Area of influence: personality.

Position in chart shows: how and where you want to shine.

Qualities: energizing, fortifying.

Associated with: ego, leadership, health, dignity, the capacity for experience, the masculine principle in everyone's makeup.

Sun in the houses

House	Interpretation
1	The Sun in this house acquires Arian characteristics and is strongly placed. Your personal affairs need much time.
2	The Sun in the second house acts like a Taurean sun. You have an ambition for material gains and are effective at acquiring things.
3	When the Sun is in the third house it has many of the communicative qualities of Gemini. You have a lively mind, and are friendly to neighbors.
4	In this house the Sun shows Cancerian qualities. You are often conservative and strongly influenced by home.
5	In the fifth house the Sun behaves like Leo, the sign it rules. This is a strong place for success, enjoyment and creativity.

Sun in the houses (continued)

House	Interpretation
6	In the sixth house the Sun acts like Virgo. You are keen to help others and dedicated to good work habits and health.
7	Here the Sun behaves similarly to a Libran Sun. Friends and enemies are the key to personality.
8	In the eighth house the Sun takes on many of Scorpio's qualities. You have a deep interest in the nature of things.
9	In the ninth house the Sun takes on Sagittarian qualities. You have high ideals, broad interests; perhaps foreign travel.
10	The Sun in the tenth house takes on some of the qualities of Capricorn. You gain purpose and have a desire for status and success.
11	The Sun in the eleventh house acts like an Aquarian. Social ambition and cooperative ventures appeal to you.
12	The Sun in the twelfth house takes on the qualities of Pisces. You are dreamy and may have difficulty expressing yourself.

Sun in the zodiac signs (continued)

Sign	Interpretation
Aries	Enterprising, headstrong, you like to have your own way, may be opinionated.
Taurus	Steadfast, persistent, you like luxury and security, a faithful friend, an implacable enemy.
Gemini	Eloquent, sensitive, restless, you love variety and change, you like to socialize, may be vague.
Cancer	Imaginative, broody, cautious, you like to feel secure, defensive when shy, home is important.
Leo	Generous, proud, confident, you stand up for yourself, like attention, can be patronizing.
Virgo	Thoughtful, cool-headed, modest, you have a strong sense of duty, may be fussy about rules.

Sign	Interpretation
Libra	Diplomatic, charming, sociable, able to compromise with others, sometimes indecisive.
Scorpio	Secretive, determined, shrewd, you like to know all that is going on, may be sharp and jealous.
Sagittarius	Tolerant, friendly, enthusiastic, you love freedom and adventure, sometimes blunt and extravagant.
Capricorn	Practical, serious, loyal, self-disciplined, you work hard to achieve, may be slow to trust others.
Aquarius	Full of new ideas, unpredictable, you like to express ideas freely, can be rebellious and distant.
Pisces	Kind to others, versatile, sensitive, you love to dream, may find it hard to be practical.

THE MOON: mirror of life

Area of influence: moods.
Position in chart shows: reflects your moods.
Qualities: nurturing, receptive.
Associated with: fertility, the need to touch, habits, desires, reflex actions, fluctuations, cycles, the feminine principle in everyone's makeup.

Moon in the houses

House	Interpretation
1	Moody, changeable, perhaps shy, imaginative, sensitive to feelings within yourself.
2	You have a great need for material security. Capable of being generous or mean, can be persuasive.
3	Curious, with a good memory but lack of long-term concentration. Dramatic, expressive, restless.
4	You feel strongly about family, parents, the home, family history, although there may be many changes.
5	May be fond of children. You have a love of theatrical effects and strong romantic emotions. Creative in cycles.

Moon in the houses (continued)

House	Interpretation
6	Can be nervous, with changeable habits. Strong desire to serve and look after people. May suffer from vague illnesses.
7	Subject to changes in friendships, generally popular, responsive to the needs of others, indecisive.
8	You need security and have an interest in love, sex and affection. May be morbid.
9	You enjoy studying the meaning of life at any level. Philosophical, with a natural ability to teach others.
10	May be constantly in the public eye. There may be many changes of occupation.
11	You take an objective view of organizations and clubs. Often have many helpful friends, sometimes false friends.
12	Often like speculaion or working alone. Retiring, uncomfortable in strange surroundings.

Moon in the zodiac signs

Sign	Interpretation
Aries	Enthusiastic, sincere, nervous asking for help, emotionally dominating, can blow hot or cold.
Taurus	Affectionate, faithful, sentimental, may be timid, emotionally steady, can be loyal or stubborn.
Gemini	May need to do several things at once, emotionally versatile, can be dispassionate.
Cancer	Can be devoted and trusting, intuitive, thrifty, easily hurt, emotionally possessive.
Leo	Romantic, honest, loving, magnetic, Emotionally bountiful, can be fiery and self-concerned.
Virgo	Can seem shy, generous, emotionally appreciative but can be emotionally demanding and insecure.

Sign	Interpretation
Libra	Affectionate and sociable, can be indecisive, Emotionally gracious, you need to be approved by others.
Scorpio	Sacrificial, proud, jealous, emotionally intense but often controlled, can be deeply hurt.
Sagittarius	Happy-go-lucky, with good judgment, can be naïve, need total freedom, emotionally idealistic.
Capricorn	Supersensitive, dignified, can be melancholic, may have great passions, emotionally inhibited.
Aquarius	Idealistic, you need outlets for tension, emotionally detached with a preference for cool friendship.
Pisces	Can be sentimental and self-pitying, emotionally subjective with an instinctive feeling for others.

MERCURY: the messenger

Area of influence: thoughts, mind.

Position in chart shows: how you best communicate.

Qualities: quick and versatile.

Influences: words and intellect, everything associated with communication, dexterity, capacity for emotion, reason, thought, local travel and activities.

Mercury in the houses

House	Interpretation
1	May find it hard to understand feelings of others, self-conscious, point of view starts from yourself.
2	Rational, value-conscious, commercial sensitivity. Point of view starts from "What can I gain?"
3	Restless and communication-conscious may ask "Where can I go, who can I meet, what can I learn?"
4	Thrifty and family conscious. Point of view begins from history, family, the home, or a need to collect.
5	Full of bright ideas, pleasure conscious, on the lookout for fun, chance, novelty, affairs.

Mercury in the houses (continued)

House	Interpretation
6	You apply thought systematically. A need to have many irons in the fire and back-up plans, conscious of duty.
7	Partnerships are important to you, people-conscious. Your point of view starts from "What can we do together?"
8	Intuitive, conscious of hidden motives, your outlook starts from "What's really going on here?"
9	Your outlook is philosophical and free ranging. Aware that there is always something new to be learned.
10	Conscious of status, your viewpoint starts from "How can these facts be used to my best advantage?"
11	Socially conscious, you are concerned with what is best for a group of people.
12	Aware of inner feelings on which you base decisions, you may be insecure or guarded.

Mercury in the zodiac signs

Sign	Interpretation
Aries	Inventive, quick, witty, direct, an impulsive mind, you can improvise, look ahead, may be impatient.
Taurus	You value facts, weigh evidence, but may have mental inertia.
Gemini	Perceptive, communicative, quick, witty, logical, with many thoughts. May not be thorough.
Cancer	Impressionable, receptive, retentive. Subjective. Arguments make you adamant.
Leo	You solve problems, speak with authority, broadminded, sometimes ignore details, may be quick-tempered.
Virgo	Sensible, methodical, practical and analytical. May be critical and impersonal.

Sign	Interpretation
Libra	Diplomatic, active, just, you look for compromise, dislike losing arguments.
Scorpio	Probing, shrewd, you rarely change opinion, which can be forcefully stated.
Sagittarius	Honest, independent, progressive, may be very direct, blunt, scatterbrained.
Capricorn	Ambitious, memory for detail, cautious, serious, dry-witted, may be satirical.
Aquarius	Observant, interest in abstract ideas, resourceful, original, may be eccentric and stubborn.
Pisces	Osmotic mind capable of exact insight, receptive, may be morbid or woolly-minded.

VENUS: the goddess of love

Area of influence: feelings.
Position in chart shows: where your values lie.
Qualities: gentle, sensuous.
Influences: pleasures, morality, affections, possessions, the arts, marriage, sociability, love.

Venus in the houses

House	Interpretation
1	Kind, happy, balanced, enjoy luxury, may like to be spoiled, you value yourself.
2	Like to work in luxurious surroundings, value own talents and possessions.
3	Dislike arguments, prefer persuasion to force, value a charming family and pleasant friendships.
4	Strong ethical values. You value a comfortable, organized home that you create yourself.
5	Value pleasure, giving pleasure to others, affection, love affairs, children, creative ventures.

Venus in the houses (continued)

House	Interpretation
6	May be a "Good Samaritan," if sometimes indulgently, value service both received and given.
7	You value social graces, harmony, the law. May be happy in business, public life or marriage.
8	May benefit greatly from others. Value sensuality and life itself. Spiritual peace may be important.
9	You enjoy travel and value enthusiasm and zeal.
10	You may be popular with associates willing to help you, and value diplomacy and status.
11	A variety of affiliations and friendships are of value to you, you may be too idealistic for a group.
12	Privacy and seclusion are important to you. You may feel an urge to serve others.

Venus in the zodiac signs

Sign	Interpretation
Aries	Outgoing, demonstrative, ardent, magnetic, you like to present yourself well, may be overwhelming.
Taurus	Love luxury and touching things, artistic, steadfast, faithful, sensual, may be possessive.
Gemini	Love to roam around freely, bright, generous, friendly. May be fickle in affection or romance.
Cancer	May have an instinct to nurture, caring, devoted, idealistic, gentle. May be too clinging.
Leo	Love life, love to be noticed, romantic, warm-hearted, lavish. May be jealous.
Virgo	Inhibited, shy, hide sensuality, undemonstrative. Can behave in exactly the opposite way.

Sign	Interpretation
Libra	May be more in love with love than with your partner. Attractive, gracious, appreciative.
Scorpio	Loyal, passionate, magnetic, can feel desolate or become cruel if rejected sexually.
Sagittarius	Deal with affection freely, idealistic, adventurous, humorous, may hate commitments.
Capricorn	Reserved on the surface, dedicated, proud, may hide fear of sensuality being rejected.
Aquarius	Friendly, cool, detached, you do not like to be tied down, may prefer platonic relationships.
Pisces	Tender, gentle, compassionate, may be self-sacrificing or hypersensitive.

MARS: the warrior

Area of influence: action, drive.

Position in chart shows: how and where energy is used.

Qualities: active, competitive.

Influences: physical movement, construction, power, courage, strength, initiative, self-assertion, sexual energy.

Mars in the houses

House	Interpretation
1	Keen to prove yourself. Competitive, practical, self-assertive. May be boisterous.
2	Energy devoted to getting rich quickly, resourceful, generous. May lose riches as quickly as they were gained.
3	Love argument and debate. Restless, impatient, assertive with words. May be tactless.
4	Energy devoted to fulfilling a need for security. May have to move from birthplace.
5	Creative, a born promoter, impulsive. Like to be up and doing. May be a bad loser. May be athletic.

Mars in the houses (continued)

House	Interpretation
6	You put energy into work and service and expect same from others. You have a passion for orderliness.
7	May be a controversial personality. You attract strong reactions from people.
8	Money is usually important. You devote energy to matters such as life, death, sex, love.
9	Often have wide-ranging ventures. May include travel and self-education.
10	Strong drive to reach top position as devoted to achievement of ambition.
11	Energy devoted to group interests, creative promotions, social affairs.
12	May behave like a passive pressure cooker or a rebel. Energy may be limited or used indirectly.

Mars in the zodiac signs

Sign	Interpretation
Aries	Sexually dynamic, energy is used for vigorous, self-willed action. You dislike timidity or routine.
Taurus	Sexually earthy. May be jealous. You use energy to plow through obtacles, like to be the boss.
Gemini	Sexually prefer variety. You use energy to quickly put ideas into action. Can sell anyone anything.
Cancer	Sexually sensitive. You use energy protectively and acquisitively. May smoulder emotionally.
Leo	You are either a winner or loser but never an also-ran. You use energy to act courageously and generously.
Virgo	Sexually shy. You use energy to develop strategies for perfection. May be more ardent in work than in love.

Mars in the zodiac signs (continued)

Sign	Interpretation
Libra	Sexually, like the sweet music and soft lights approach. You use energy to fight for peace.
Scorpio	Sexually you demand all or nothing. Explosive energy from vast hidden resources.
Sagittarius	You sometimes burn the candle at both ends. Use energy for a perpetual love affair with life.
Capricorn	Sexually persistent. You use energy to sustain effort. May speak softly and carry a big stick.
Aquarius	Sexually innovative. You use energy to galvanize breakups, breakdowns, and breakthroughs.
Pisces	Romantic and sensual. You dislike physical action. Under pressure, energy remains inward.

JUPITER: the prophet

Area of influence: expansion and freedom.
Position in chart shows: where your opportunities for improvement lie.
Qualities: broadminded, optimistic, benevolent, philosophical.
Influences: growth, long distance travel, prosperity.

Jupiter in the houses

House	Interpretation
1	Optimistic, humorous, breezy, broad-minded, an executive type. Could become self-indulgent.
2	Likable, prosperous, a business type. Could be showy or spendthrift.
3	Happy-go-lucky, witty, with good relations with the public, students or relatives.
4	You like to entertain and be in control. Outgoing, generous, loyal, head-of-the-family type.
5	Happy-family type, you have wide interests, dramatic, gamble—win if not too reckless.

Jupiter in the houses (continued)

House	Interpretation
6	Lucky, cheerful, you enjoy your work. The kind of person for whom something always turns up.
7	You live a happy life, often gaining from others. Like to lavish affection on partner.
8	Liking to manage the affairs of others, you are discerning and resourceful with a positive attitude to life and sex.
9	Devoted, tolerant, faithful, you get along with people from other religions and cultures.
10	A leader, ambitious, proud, self-reliant, trustworthy. Could become overbearing.
11	You devote time to people and enjoy social contacts. Benevolent, with high aspirations.
12	Resourceful in trouble, kind, you like to give in secret, perhaps because you doubt yourself.

Jupiter in the zodiac signs

Sign	Interpretation
Aries	You use opportunities to the fullest extent to improve yourself. May become egocentric.
Taurus	You use opportunities to improve the value of money and the luxury it can buy. Dissipation can result from extravagance.
Gemini	An alert, fun-loving person full of ideas. Can be temperamental.
Cancer	You use opportunities to share generously and to improve relations with a wide public. May become overly sentimental.
Leo	You use opportunities to improve conditions by making someone's dream come true. May be arrogant or exuberant.
Virgo	You improve standards by attention to detail. May be lazy or make mountains out of molehills.

Sign	Interpretation
Libra	You improve leisure time and pleasures, especially with a partner. You are hospitable. Hopeless alone.
Scorpio	You improve life by thinking big and doing work to match. Shrewd. Can be uncompromising.
Sagittarius	Always optimistic, you use opportunities to make life brighter for others. May be reckless.
Capricorn	You expand through economy, hard work and dedication. Can be a martyr or too orthodox.
Aquarius	You use opportunities to help people regardless of their religion or race. Can be revolutionary. May be unrealistic.
Pisces	You use opportunities to improve the lot of the underdog, quietly and unassumingly. Can be too self-sacrificing.

SATURN: the lawgiver

Area of influence: Responsibility.
Position in chart shows: how and where you compensate against insecurity.
Qualities: persistent, wise, truthful.
Influences: ambition, capacity for a career, aging, responsibility.

Saturn in the houses

House	Interpretation
1	Saturn in the first house indicates that a sense of personal inadequacy may spur you on.
2	Saturn in the second house suggests that anxiety is due to possessions, money, or lack of money.
3	Fear of being lonely or of the unknown is characterized by Saturn in the third house.
4	Anxiety about being a nobody, or about age is characterized by Saturn in the fourth house.
5	People with Saturn in the fifth house may have anxiety about expressing themselves fully.

Saturn in the houses (continued)

House	Interpretation
6	A worrier, anxious to prove your worth has Saturn in the sixth house.
7	Saturn in the seventh house suggests difficulties in one-to-one relationships.
8	Sex and love can be sources of anxiety when Saturn is in the eighth house.
9	Anxiety may be caused by new places or new ideas.
10	Anxiety is caused by irresponsible power.
11	Anxiety can be caused by being given or offered affection.
12	Isolation can be caused by anxiousness about life.

Saturn in the zodiac signs

Sign	Interpretation
Aries	Able to use ingenuity to develop strength of character. Cooperation and tact may need to be learnt.
Taurus	Able to demonstrate patience and trustworthiness in everyday affairs. Values may need reassessing.
Gemini	In scientific pursuits can be systematic and adaptable. Spontaneity may need to be learnt.
Cancer	May be loyal to family or firm, shrewd and able. There is a need to control emotions and self-pity.
Leo	Could be a self-assured leader in any field. Sometimes need to learn to enjoy life and laughter.
Virgo	In detailed work, could be precise and prudent. May need to learn what is important.

Sign	Interpretation
Libra	Able to be made responsible for work requiring justice and good planning. Tolerance may need to be learnt.
Scorpio	Able to use subtle, strong willpower to achieve success. May need to learn to forgive and forget.
Sagittarius	You are able to build a reputation for being morally outspoken. May need to be less self-righteous.
Capricorn	Able to organize well and use power and pretige responsibly. May need to relax.
Aquarius	Capable of original abstract thought. May need to learn to express gratitude.
Pisces	You are able to demonstrate humility and understanding when working with others. May need to keep track of reality.

URANUS: the awakener

Area of influence: change and freedom.

Position in chart shows: how character is associated with ideas and the unexpected. House position shows where you behave out of character.

Qualities: originality, humanitarianism.

Influences: the will, science and magic.

A generation planet.

Uranus in the houses

House	Interpretation
1	A nonconformist you are often ahead of your time and therefore always out of character compared to your peers.
2	You invent your own value systems in an attempt to match your need for independence.
3	Inventive and unpredictable you are open-minded and behave out of character, often with genius.
4	You have a changeable home life and may like frequent changes of residence. You fear being alone.
5	With regard to established conventions (e.g. rules, marriage, children) you may act out of character.

Uranus in the houses (continued)

House	Interpretation
6	Often highly strung, you are prone to minor illnesses and sudden upsets. Must work in your own way.
7	In partnerships or personal relationships you may be unpredictable or behave in an unusual way.
8	You like to experiment and may experience unexpected or unconventional events concerning sex or money.
9	In legal matters or while traveling you may enjoy the unexpected. You are independent and unorthodox.
10	Unusual things relate to your career and work. You are altruistic, a great fighter but a bad follower.
11	You are likely to make unusual friendships and may have strange, nonconformist ideas.
12	Unconscious conflicts may surface unexpectedly. You may have secret or unusual love affairs.

Uranus in the zodiac signs

Sign	Interpretation
Aries c.1928–1934	Taking charge of life and destiny, an impetuous, self-willed pioneer.
Taurus c.1935–1942	Liable to unexpected trouble, you are nevertheless practical, determined, a builders of economic reforms.
Gemini c.1942–1949	Inventive and brilliant, with original ideas for innovative reforms. Often fickle.
Cancer c.1949–1956	Seeking freedom in marriage, in the home, and for women. Emotionally restive.
Leo c.1956–1962	Determined to change what does not suit you, using new rhythms and an unconventional outlook.
Virgo c.1962–1968	Down-to-earth, enquiring interest in advanced technology, ecology, and health.

Sign	Interpretation
Libra c.1968–1975	Magnetic and charming, out to give meaning to relationships and rectify injustices.
Scorpio c.1891–1898; 1975–1981	Seeking new approaches, decisive, fascinating, daring, and intense.
Sagittarius c.1898–1904; 1981–1988	With a progressive, open mind, equable and optimistic.
Capricorn c.1905–1912; 1988–1995	Determined to reconcile conflicts, resourceful and responsible.
Aquarius c.1912–1919; 1995–2002	Although sometimes impractical, a free thinker, strong, humanitarian, and inventive.
Pisces c.1919–1927	Although sometimes escapist or impractical, nevertheless visionary, imaginative and often self-sacrificing.

NEPTUNE: the mystic

Area of influence: imagination and intuition.

Position in chart shows: how character is associated with a spiritual or escapist urge. House position shows self-deceptive or idealistic trends.

Qualities: subtlety, mystery.

Influences: illusions (including drugs),
A generation planet.

Neptune in the houses

House	Interpretation
1	You have a strong imagination and are charismatic but may idealize yourself because you do not see yourself clearly.
2	Intuitive with a sense of value, you may be impractical with money and idealize possessions.
3	Intuitive and persuasive, you dream about your idealistic world. You may feel misunderstood or vague.
4	Musical and artistic, you are uncertain about your own identity but idealize home or family.
5	Highly creative, you need lots of romantic affairs and idealize romance and the people you love.

Neptune in the houses (continued)

House	Interpretation
6	Sensitive, lonely, and poetic, you idealize about whatever you do but may suffer vague illnesses or simply drift along.
7	Often influenced by or serving others, you idealize others in your life but may need to face realities.
8	Intuitive and charismatic you idealize the search for truth but may lead others or yourself astray.
9	Intellectual and tolerant, you idealize educational and social reforms but may be impressionable.
10	With an awareness of emotions and high aspirations, you idealize your public image but may have self-doubts.
11	Intuitive and generous you idealize those who are different or odd but may be unreliable.
12	A loner, you are wise but sensitive and idealize insight. You may deceive yourself or be deceived.

Neptune in the zodiac signs

Sign	Interpretation
Aries c.1861–1874	Pioneers of new philosopphical ideas, radical missionaries with a strong ego.
Taurus c.1874–1887	With an instinct for business, experimental and artistic, but sometimes led astray by others.
Gemini c.1887–1901	With new ideas on communications, trade, and travel. Enquiring, alert, and restless.
Cancer c.1901–1915	Despite upheavals, strong ties to family and home. Mystical, emotional, and patriotic.
Leo c.1915–1929	Bringing new developments, flair, and idealization. Powerful, speculative, and romantic.
Virgo c.1929–1943	Humanitarians divided between reason and emotion. May throw the baby out with the bathwater.

Sign	Interpretation
Libra c.1943–1956	"Doing their own thing" causes problems. Peace loving and compassionate, may be impractical.
Scorpio c.1956–1970	An interest in new approaches, both good and bad. Emotional and investigative.
Sagittarius c.1970–1984	New universal ideals and things previously hidden are revealed as the result of frankness.
Capricorn c.1984–1998	Conscientious, conventional, and practical, a period of applied knowledge.
Aquarius c.1998–2012	A philosophical outlook and detached attitude mark this as the start of a peaceful period.
Pisces c.1847–1861	A period of new cultural concepts.

PLUTO: the dark lord

Area of influence: transformation.

Position in chart shows: that which is hidden. House position shows the complexities you have to resolve alone.

Qualities: ruler of the underworld.

Influences: birth, death, atomic power, group processes. A generation planet.

Pluto in the houses

House	Interpretation
1	Pluto in the first house indicates a desire to resolve the complete expression of the many sides of your strong, creative personality.
2	Pluto in the second house indicates the desire to prevent assets ruining your happiness, and to turn liabilities into assets.
3	Pluto in the third house suggests a desire to face changes in your life, resolve your shortcoming, and make yourself heard.
4	In this house, Pluto represents an urge to identify and resolve the complexities of your origins, and to transform yourself.
5	Here Pluto reveals your urge to take risks and resolve your strong creative, emotional and erotic feelings.

Pluto in the houses (continued)

House	Interpretation
6	Pluto in the sixth house suggests a desire to resolve your mission in life in your own individualistic way.
7	A desire to use your dynamic personality to resolve issues of interpersonal circumstances is revealed by Pluto in this house.
8	Your urge to investigate and resolve hidden desires, obsessions and mysteries (yours and those of others) is revealed by Pluto in this house.
9	Pluto in the ninth house indicates an adventurous urge to resolve a dream by trying everything life has to offer.
10	Pluto in the tenth house suggests the desire to resolve a need to assert yourself and gain identity or acclaim.
11	An intense desire to reform the world single-handed is revealed by Pluto in the eleventh house.
12	In this house, Pluto indicates your urge to change personal limitations or resolve inner fears and frustrations.

Pluto in the zodiac signs

Sign	Interpretation
Aries c.1823–1851	With imagination, daring, and initiative, and a desire for revenge, reform, or power.
Taurus c.1851–1883	A great need for permanence, wealth, and security. With growth of materialism.
Gemini c.1883–1913	Critical, impetuous, and intellectual, this is a time for major changes through new inventions.
Cancer c.1913–1938	With social awareness and a need for security, a period of patriotism, pride, and great upheaval.
Leo c.1938–1957	A period when power was sought and developed, with business skill, perversity, and self-confidence.
Virgo c.1957–1971	Perfecting, analytical and inventive, this was a period of intense technical development.

Sign	Interpretation
Libra c.1971–1983	Responsible, adaptable, but fickle, a time of social change inspired by justice.
Scorpio c.1983–1995	A period that was innovative and may be redemptive. Environmental sensitivity.
Sagittarius c.1995–?	With a return to fundamental laws, this period is predicted to be reformative.
Capricorn	With an emphasis on management and organization this is a predicted period of ambition and efficiency.
Aquarius	Pluto in Aquarius predicts a period of love, freedom, and revelation. Also indicated are ingeniousness, revolution, and unconventionalism.
Pisces	Pluto in Pisces predicts the next period of enlightenment in human history, a period of compassion and sensitivity.

SIGNS OF THE ZODIAC

Each sign of the zodiac has a name, symbol, quality, element, and ruling planet.

Using this element of the birth chart it is possible to answer "How?" questions. For example, it is possible to

Sign	Symbol	Name
Aries	♈	Ram
Taurus	♉	Bull
Gemini	♊	Twins
Cancer	♋	Crab
Leo	♌	Lion
Virgo	♍	Virgin

discover how imaginative a person is by locating the sign in which Neptune is placed (the planet whose area of influence is imagination).

Quality	Element	Ruler	
Cardinal	Fire	Mars	♂
Fixed	Earth	Venus	♀
Mutable	Air	Mercury	☿
Cardinal	Water	Moon	☽
Fixed	Fire	Sun	☉
Mutable	Earth	Mercury	☿

Continued

SIGNS OF THE ZODIAC (continued)

Sign	Symbol	Name
Libra	♎	Scales
Scorpio	♏	Scorpion
Sagittarius	♐	Archer
Capricorn	♑	Goat
Aquarius	♒	Waterman
Pisces	♓	Fishes

Quality	Element	Ruler	
Cardinal	Air	Venus	♀
Fixed	Water	Pluto	♇
Mutable	Fire	Jupiter	♃
Cardinal	Earth	Saturn	♄
Fixed	Air	Uranus	♅
Mutable	Water	Neptune	♆

Qualities of the signs
One of three qualities is attributed to each sign.

Quality	Describes	Signs
Cardinal	Signs which use their abilities to achieve ambitions.	Aries Cancer Libra Capricorn
	♈ ♋ ♎ ♑	
Fixed	Signs which hold on to what they have and resist change.	Taurus Leo Scorpio Aquarius
	♉ ♌ ♏ ♒	
Mutable	Signs which are always searching and often changing.	Gemini Virgo Sagittarius Pisces
	♊ ♍ ♐ ♓	

The four elements

One of four elements is attributed to each sign.

Element	Description	Signs
Fire ♈ ♌ ♐	A process, not a substance, fire is glowing and volcanic, difficult to contain. Once burning, fire will use up air, boil water, or scorch earth.	Aries Leo Sagittarius
Earth ♉ ♍ ♑	Earth can be used for planting or building, solid or sandy, it can channel water, make a fireplace, and coexist with air.	Taurus Virgo Capricorn
Air ♊ ♎ ♒	Always on the move and invisible, air is windy or balmy; it rises above earth, makes bubbles in water, and is transformed by fire, to which it is essential.	Gemini Libra Aquarius
Water ♋ ♏ ♓	Water seeks its own level, can be clear or muddy, can evaporate, freeze, and reflect rainbows; it can put out a fire, flood earth, and dampen air.	Cancer Scorpio Pisces

Combining qualities and elements

Combining qualities and elements gives an indication of a sign's positive and negative qualities.

Sign	Positive characteristics	Negative characteristics
Aries ♈	Dynamic Independent	Hasty Arrogant
Taurus ♉	Stable Loyal	Stubborn Possessive
Gemini ♊	Communicative Adaptable	Gossipy Scheming
Cancer ♋	Sensitive Sympathetic	Touchy Manipulative
Leo ♌	Generous Self-assured	Pretentious Pompous
Virgo ♍	Humane Discriminating	Insular Petty

Sign	Positive characteristics	Negative characteristics
Libra ♎	Diplomatic Refined	Fickle Apathetic
Scorprio ♏	Passionate Probing	Jealous Suspicious
Sagittarius ♐	Honest Enthusiastic	Blunt Big-headed
Capricorn ♑	Economical Responsible	Mean Inhibited
Aquarius ♒	Just Altruistic	Two-faced Vague
Pisces ♓	Intuitive Sacrificing	Unreliable Lazy

THE HOUSES

To each of the houses is attributed a quality, an element, and an area of everyday life.

House	Quality	Element	Area of everyday life
1	Angular	Life	Identiy and outlook
2	Succedent	Purpose	Values and freedom
3	Cadent	Relationships	Awareness and contact
4	Angular	Endings	Security and home
5	Succedent	Life	Creativity and children
6	Cadent	Purpose	Work and service

House	Quality	Element	Area of everyday life
7	Angular	Relationships	Marriage and partnership
8	Succedent	Endings	Regeneration and sex
9	Cadent	Life	Aspiration and beliefs
10	Angular	Purpose	Honor and status
11	Succedent	Relationships	Friends and hopes
12	Cadent	Endings	Subconscious secrets

Qualities of the houses

Each of the houses is attributed one of three qualities.

Quality	Houses
ANGULAR These houses are where action is initiated.	1 4 7 10
SUCCEDENT In these houses action is stabilized.	2 5 8 11
CADENT In these houses we learn from actions and adapt.	3 6 9 12

Elements of the houses

To each of the houses is attributed one of four elements.

HOUSES OF LIFE

If you have several planets in these houses you have boundless energy, enthusiasm and conviction.

House	Represents
First house	Physical energy
Fifth house	Creative energy
Ninth house	Spiritual energy

HOUSES OF PURPOSE

If you have several planets in these houses you are stable, reliable, and practical.

House	Represents
Second house	Possessions and finances
Sixth house	Occupation
Tenth house	Recognition

HOUSES OF RELATIONSHIPS

If you have several planets in these houses you need other people.

House	Represents
Third house	Chance relationships
Seventh house	Close relationships
Eleventh house	Social relationships

HOUSES OF ENDINGS

If you have several planets in these houses you are sensitive to the way in which we may attain freedom.

House	Represents
Fourth house	Letting go of physical security
Eighth house	Enlightenment of the mind
Twelfth house	Release from secret fears

Overview of the qualities and elements relating to zodiac signs

ELEMENT	QUALITY		
	Cardinal	Fixed	Mutable
Fire	♈ Aries	♌ Leo	♐ Sagittarius
Earth	♑ Capricorn	♉ Taurus	♍ Virgo
Air	♎ Libra	♒ Aquarius	♊ Gemini
Water	♋ Cancer	♏ Scorpio	♓ Pisces

Overview of the qualities and areas of interest of the houses

AREA OF INTEREST	QUALITY		
	Angular	Succedent	Cadent
Life	1	5	9
Purpose	10	2	6
Relationship	7	11	3
Endings	4	8	12

DIGNITIES

More information can be gleaned from your birth chart
with additional analysis of the position of planets. The
terms "dignity," "detriment," "exaltation," and "fall"
are used to describe the positions of planets relative to
the signs in which they are placed. Following this
explanation of terms is a table of dignities showing all
the planets and how they are affected by their sign
placements.

Dignity

Planets are said to be in dignity when they are in the
sign of which they are the natural ruler: Mars rules
Aries; Venus rules Taurus and Libra; Mercury rules
Gemini and Virgo; the moon rules Cancer; the sun rules
Leo; Pluto rules Scorpio; Jupiter rules Sagittarius;
Saturn rules Capricorn; Uranus rules Aquarius;
Neptune rules Pisces.

If you have a planet in dignity, you control the
conditions in that part of your chart.

You will see from the table of dignities that Aquarius,
Pisces and Scorpio are shown to be ruled by Saturn,
Jupiter and Mars. This is because these planets were
their rulers until Uranus, Neptune and Pluto were
discovered. Saturn, Jupiter and Mars are therefore
sometimes called the old rulers with reference to
Aquarius, Pisces and Scorpio.

Some astronomers believe that there are two other planets still to be discovered in our solar system and that these will become rulers of Virgo and Libra.

Detriment

This is the opposite to dignity. It occurs when a planet is in the sign opposite the one it would naturally rule.

If you have a planet in detriment, you must accept the conditions in that part of your chart.

Exaltation

A planet is exalted when it is in a sign from which it draws its source of power.

You feel very positive and happy in that part of your chart where you have a planet in exaltation.

Fall

When other signs restrict a planet's power, the planet is said to be in fall.

A planet in fall indicates an area of your chart where you feel ill at ease.

Mutual reception

Planets are said to be in mutual reception when they are in one another's zodiac signs. Under these circumstances the energies of both planets are emphasized as they work together.

Table of dignities

Planet	Dignity	Detriment
Sun	Leo	Aquarius
Moon	Cancer	Capricorn
Mercury	Gemini, Virgo	Sagittarius Pisces
Venus	Taurus, Libra	Scorpio, Aries
Mars	Aries, Scorpio	Libra, Taurus
Jupiter	Sagittarius, Pisces	Gemini, Virgo
Saturn	Capricorn, Aquarius	Cancer, Leo
Uranus	Aquarius	Leo
Neptune	Pisces	Virgo
Pluto	Scorpio	Taurus

Exaltation	Fall	Planet
Aries	Libra	Sun
Taurus	Scorpio	Moon
Virgo, Aquarius	Pisces	Mercury
Pisces	Virgo	Venus
Capricorn	Cancer	Mars
Cancer	Capricorn	Jupiter
Libra	Aries	Saturn
Scorpio	Taurus	Uranus
Cancer	Capricorn	Neptune
Pisces	Virgo	Pluto

ASPECTS

Another important component of the birth chart is the angle between planets, known as aspects. They are important to identify and interpret because they provide useful information about areas of the personality represented by the planets. Aspects are neither good nor bad; they simply show where adjustments have to be made between different parts of the personality in action, or where parts are challenged or emphasized. Each aspect has a different symbol, illustrated below.

Aspects

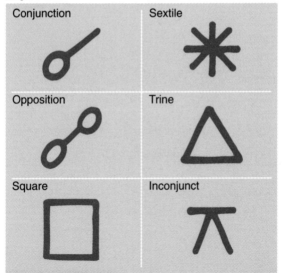

Conjunction	Sextile
Opposition	Trine
Square	Inconjunct

The six major aspects

There are six major aspects (shown below) thought to be of considerable importance because they describe the relationships between all the elements and qualities of the zodiac signs. Besides the name and symbol representing each aspect (angle), each also has an orb—the number of degrees of deviation allowed from the exact angle of the aspect—and a special meaning. On the next few pages they are described and information provided about how to locate and interpret them on the birth chart.

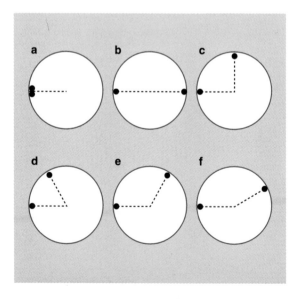

INTERPRETATION OF THE MAJOR ASPECTS

Aspect	Description
Conjunction	Planets in the same sign act in the same way and concentrate their energies.
Opposition	Conflict between opposite signs produces a potential for self-awareness and perspective.
Square	Tension between the elemental ways in which two planets operate offers a challenge.

Angle	Orb	Meaning
0°	7°	Concentration
180°	7°	Perspective
90°	7°	Challenge

INTERPRETATION OF THE MAJOR ASPECTS

Aspect	Description
Sextile	Planets placed in compatible signs offer opportunities.
Trine	A satisfying, easy combination of planets.
Inconjunct	Planets suggest a need to reorganize or reconcile parts of the self.

(continued)

Angle	Orb	Meaning
60°	**5°**	Opportunity
120°	**7°**	Satisfaction
150°	**5°**	Reorganization

Signs in opposition

The list below shows the "good" and "bad" polarities that can exist within each sign's identity. It is essential to know these when considering signs in opposition. Signs are shown here with their identities, alongside their opposites.

Sign	Identity	Sign	Identity
Aries	I exist Me first	Libra	I cooperate I procrastinate
Taurus	I have I indulge	Scorpio	I desire I suspect
Gemini	I think I scheme	Sagitarrius	I understand I exaggerate
Cancer	I feel I brood	Capricorn	I use I inhibit
Leo	I will I pretend	Aquarius	I know I'm unreliable
Virgo	I study I worry	Pisces	I believe I escape

House opposites

Although houses are never *in opposition*, they do have their opposites. By looking at the positioning of aspects in the houses it is possible to identify the area of life to which that aspect applies. Never take meanings literally. Security, for example, may mean financial secruty, emotional security, physical security, etc.

House	Areas	House	Areas
1	Myself Outlook	7	Yourself Partnerships
2	What is mine Values	8	What is yours Investments
3	Life here and near Awareness	9	Life there and far Optimism and learning
4	Private life/ source Security	10	Public life/ image Status
5	What I give Creativity	11	What I receive Ideas
6	Physical health Service	12	Mental health Secrets

Three or more planets in the same aspect

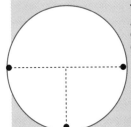

T-Square
A T-square is formed when one planet is square to two others in the chart.

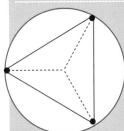

Grand trine
Three planets in trine aspect form a grand trine, an aspect of ease, pleasure, and harmony.

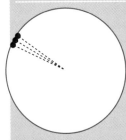

The stellium
Three or more planets lying within seven degrees of each other on the chart are called a stellium, and indicate individuality or a special interest.

Squares
Grand square
When four planets in opposition are square to each other, they form the most powerful aspect that can be found on any chart, the grand square (sometimes called the grand cross).

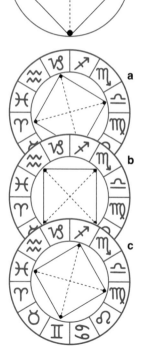

Squares and oppositions
These are always aspects between planets in cardinal (**a**), fixed (**b**), or mutable (**c**) signs. Squares indicate turning points, potential accomplishments, or disruptions. They suggest action to be taken as a result of life's challenges. Oppositions give perspective and can be areas of conflict or cooperation. Cardinal aspects operate quickly, with the intention of solving problems. Fixed aspects may show an acceptance of the situation. They are slow and deliberate. Mutable aspects are often influenced by other people and indicate variable actions.

Trines and sextiles

Trines

Trine aspects of 120° indicate stability, ease, and a general feeling of satisfaction and joy. They are always

Earth trines
These are found in charts of practical realists.

Water trines
People with water trines experience every shade of feeling and may be very intuitive.

Sextiles

These are aspects of 60° and offer a great deal of opportunity for self-expression. They occur between a

Planets in fire and air signs.

between signs of one element. However, several trines on a chart may not be beneficial.

Air trines
Individuals with air trines are given to much thought and idealism.

Fire trines
People with fire trines are naturally energetic.

planet in a fire sign and a planet in an air sign or a planet in an earth sign and a planet in a water sign.

Planets in earth and water signs.

Conjunctions

These concentrate energy and occur when planets are
within 7° of each other. The example below shows an
exact conjunction and a stellium.

An exact conjunction

Here Neptune and the Moon are in exact conjunction at
28° of Virgo (**1**), indicating someone who has difficulty
telling illusion from reality, who is sensitive and
impressionable.

A stellium

A stellium of Uranus, Venus, and Saturn occurs in this
charts at 2°, 3°, and 9° respectively of Gemini (**2**). This
suggests a person who is fickle, original, detached, with
some genius, but who perhaps has a need for security.
Saturn's presence suggests that duty and happiness are
seen as synonymous.

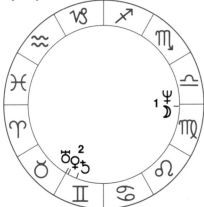

Inconjuncts

Inconjunct aspects between signs are easy to locate: a sign is inconjunct with the sign each side of its opposite. Our example shows that Aries can be inconjunct with both Scorpio and Virgo, or with one of them. These are always aspects between signs that have neither qualities nor elements in common. Consequently they may indicate areas where an adjustment or some reorganization has to take place. Inconjuncts are always aspects between signs that have neither qualities nor elements in common. In our example, the cardinal fire sign Aries has nothing in common with either the fixed water sign Scorpio or the mutable earth sign Virgo. The more exact the angle, the greater the strain between elements. An exact angle of 150°, for example, suggests considerable habit-changing or re-thinking is necessary.

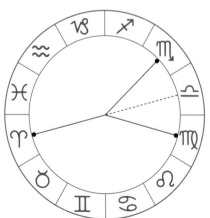

FORTUNE-TELLING GLOSSARY

Aeromancy
Divination by atmospheric conditions. There are
several different forms, including austromancy,
ceraunoscopy, chaomancy, and meteormancy.

Ailuromancy
Divination from cats.

Alectryomancy
A form of augury, in this case divination from the
eating patterns of sacred chickens.

Aleuromancy
Divination using slips of paper baked in dough balls.
The modern equivalent are Chinese fortune cookies.

Alphitomancy
Divination using cakes made of wheat or barley flour.

Arachnomancy
A form of augury, in this case divination from the
appearance and behavior of spiders.

Arithomancy
A form of divination in which numbers are believed to
exert an influence on our lives and personality. This is
also called numerology or numeromancy.

Astragalomancy
A form of sortilege which in this case is divination
using the bones of sheep.

Astrology
Divination using stars and planets and involving signs
of the zodiac (e.g. Aries, Taurus, Gemini, etc).

Augury
Divination based mainly on the appearance and
behavior of animals and includes alectryomancy,
arachnomancy, cephalomancy, entomomancy,
ichthyomancy, myomancy, ophiomancy, scapulomancy,
and zoomancy, and also oenomancy and tephromancy.
Haruspicy is sometimes considered part of augury.

Austromancy
A form of aeromancy, in this case divination using the
wind.

Belomancy
A form of sortilege which in this case is divination by
arrows.

Bibliomancy
A form of sortilege which in this case is divination from
books and which includes rhapsodomancy. It is also
called stichomancy.

Botanomancy
A form of pyromancy which in this case is divination
by burning leaves and branches.

Capnomancy
A form of pyromancy which in this case is divination
by smoke.

Cartomancy
Divination using modern playing cards.

Catoptromancy
A form of scrying which in this case involves
divination by gazing into a mirror.

Causinomancy
A form of pyromancy which in this case is divination
by objects cast into the fire.

Cephalomancy
A form of augury, in this case divination from the skull
or head of a donkey or goat.

Ceraunoscopy
A form of aeromancy, in this case divination using
thunder and lightning.

Ceromancy
Divination from melted wax.

Chaomancy
A form of aeromancy, in this case divination using
aerial visions.

Chirognomy
Divination using the palm of the hand but which also
includes an analysis of hand shape, fingers, and
fingernails. It is also called chirology, chiromancy, and
palmistry.

Chirology
Divination using the palm of the hand but which also includes an analysis of hand shape, fingers, and fingernails. It is also called chirgnomy, chiromancy, or palmistry.

Chiromancy
Divination using the palm of the hand but which also includes an analysis of hand shape, fingers, and fingernails. It is also called chirgnomy, chirology, or palmistry.

Clairaudience
A form of clairvoyance which in this case is hearing the future ahead of time.

Clairvoyance
Divination by seeing the future ahead of time. There are many different forms of clairvoyance, including clairaudience, metagnomy, precognition, and psychometry.

Cleidomancy
A form of radiesthesia which in this case is divination using a suspended key. It may be used in dowsing.

Cleromancy
An alternative name for sortilege.

Coscinomancy
A form of radiesthesia which in this case is divination using a suspended sieve.

Crithomancy
Divination using the markings on freshly baked bread.

Cromniomancy
Divination using onions.

Crystallomancy
A form of scrying which in this case involves divination with a crystal ball.

Dactylomancy
A form of radiesthesia which in this case is divination using a suspended ring. Dactylomancy may be used in dowsing.

Daphnomancy
A form of pyromancy which in this case is divination by the burning of laurel leaves.

Dowsing
A method of divination used to locate things under the earth, including water, mineral deposits, bodies, archeological sites, cables, pipes, tunnels, lost property, or hidden treasure. Dowsing may involve radiesthesia.

Entomomancy
A form of augury which in this case is divination from the appearance and behavior of insects.

Geomancy
Divination by the earth. This can mean use of actual earth or of earthlike substances such as sand.

Graphology
A method of assessing a person's character from handwriting.

Halomancy
A form of pyromancy which in this case is divination by casting salt into a fire.

Haruspicy
Divination from the entrails of animals, one form of which is hepatoscopy. It is sometimes considered part of augury.

Hepatoscopy
A form of haruspicy which in this case is divination using the liver.

Hippomancy
Divination from horses.

Hydromancy
A form of scrying which in this case is divination by water. Pegomancy is a form of hydromancy.

I Ching
An ancient Chinese text (also known as the Book of Changes) from which one's fortune can be predicted.

Ichthyomancy
A form of augury which in this case is divination from the shape and entrails of fish.

Lampadomancy
Divination using a single oil lamp or a torch flame.

Lithomancy
Divination using precious stones.

Lychnomancy
Divination from the flames of three wax candles.

Metagnomy
A form of clairvoyance which in this case is seeing future events when in a hypnotic trance.

Meteormancy
A form of aeromancy, in this case divination using meteors and shooting stars.

Metoposcopy
A method of assessing character and fortune from lines on the forehead.

Moleoscopy
A method of assessing character from moles on the body.

Molybdomancy
Divination using molten tin or lead.

Myomancy
A form of augury which in this case is divination from the color and movement of mice.

Necromancy
A process which involves asking the dead to answer questions about the future using automatic writing, a ouija board, or through a medium.

Numerology
A form of divination in which numbers are believed to exert an influence on our lives and personality. This is also called numeromancy or arithomancy.

Numeromancy
A form of divination in which numbers are believed to exert an influence on our lives and personality. This is also called numerology or arithomancy.

Oenomancy
A form of augury which in this case is divination from the patterns made by wine.

Oneiromancy
Divination using dreams.

Ophiomancy
A form of augury which in this case is divination from the color and movement of snakes.

Oriental astrology
A form of Eastern divination based on a 12-year cycle and involving 12 animals which, unlike the zodiac signs of Western astrology, are not based on the configuration or movement of planets or stars.

Ornithomancy
Divination using the sound, appearance, and flight of
birds.

Palmistry
Divination using the palm of the hand but which also
includes an analysis of hand shape, fingers, and
fingernails. It is also called chirognomy, chirology, or
chiromancy.

Pegomancy
A form of hydromancy which in this case is divination
using a sacred pool or spring.

Pessomancy
A form of sortilege which in this case is divination by
drawing or casting of specially marked pebbles. This is
also called psephomancy.

Phyllorhodomancy
Divination using rose petals.

Phrenology
Assessing character from the presence of bumps on the
head.

Physiognomy
Character analysis using facial features.

Psephomancy
A form of sortilege which in this case is divination by
the drawing or casting of specially marked pebbles.
This is also called pessomancy.

Precognition
A form of clairvoyance which in this case is an inner paranormal knowledge of the future.

Psychometry
A form of clairvoyance which in this case involves divination about a specific person, brought about by holding an object belonging to them.

Pyromancy
Divination by fire. There are many different forms, including, botanomancy, capnomancy, causinomancy, daphnomancy, halomancy, pyroscopy, and sideromancy.

Pyroscopy
A form of pyromancy, which in this case is divination by burning a sheet of paper on a white surface and examining the resulting stains.

Radiesthesia
Using a pendulum for divination. There are different forms, including cleidomancy, coscinomancy, and dactylomancy. Radiesthesia is often used when dowsing.

Rhapsodomancy
A form of bibliomancy which in this case is divination from a book of poetry.

Runes
The symbols of an ancient alphabet that are used for divination.

Scapulomancy
A form of augury which in this case is divination from the patterns or cracks and fissures on the burned shoulder blade of an animal.

Scrying
Divination by gazing into a reflective surface. There are many different forms, including crystallomancy, catoptromancy, and hydromancy.

Sideromancy
A form of pyromancy which in this case is divination by casting an odd number of straws onto iron brought to red heat in a fire and reading the patterns formed by straws, their movements, and the nature or the flames and smoke.

Sortilege
Divination by the casting or drawing of lots. There are many different types, including astragalomancy, belomancy, bibliomancy, pessomancy (also known as psephomancy), rhapsodomancy, and stichomancy. It is also called cleromancy.

Stichomancy
A form of sortilege which in this case is divination using books. This is also called bibliomancy. Rhapsodomancy is a form of stichomancy.

Tasseography
Divination using tea leaves.

Tephromancy
Divination using the patterns formed in the ashes of burnt offerings made to the gods.

Tyromancy
Divination from cheese.

Zoomancy
A form of augury which in this case is divination from the appearance and behavior of any animal.

FORTUNE FINDER

This list can be used in two ways. First, it can be of use if you know what a particular method of fortune-telling involves but can't remember its name. For example, let's say you know that the method involves bones, but you can't remember what sort of bones or the name of the method of divination you have in mind. Looking up "bones" in the list gives you the name of three possible methods: astragalomancy, cephalomancy, and scapulomancy. You can then look these up in the glossary for a quick definition, or you can turn to them in the main body of the book.

Second, if you have an interest in a particular type of fortune telling, the list can be used to help identify related methods. For example, you could look up "Animals," "The body," or "Fire," and will find a list of related methods which you could then investigate further.

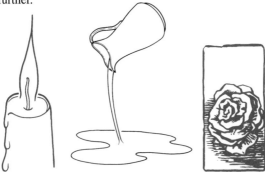

What does the method involve?	See:
Aerial visions	Chaomancy
Ancient alphabet	Runes
Animals	Ailuromancy
	Alectryomancy
	Arachnomancy
	Astragalomancy
	Cephalomancy
	Entomomancy
	Haruspicy
	Hippomancy
	Ichthyomancy
	Myomancy
	Ophiomancy
	Oriental astrology
	Ornithomancy
	Scapulomancy
	Zoomancy
Arrows	Belomancy
Ash	Pyroscopy
	Tephromancy
Atmospheric conditions	Aeromancy
	Austromancy
	Ceraunoscopy

What does the method involve?	See:
Atmospheric conditions (continued)	Chaormancy Meteormancy
Birds	Ornithomancy
The body	Chirognomy Chirology Chiromancy Metoposcopy Moleoscopy Palmistry Phrenology Physiognomy

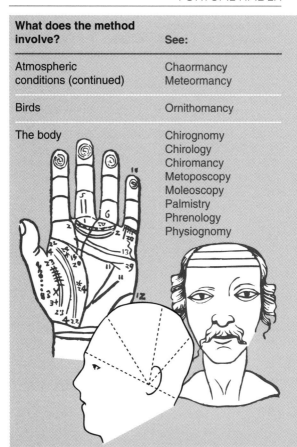

What does the method involve?	See:
Bones	Astragalomancy Cephalomancy Scapulomancy
Books	Bibliomancy I Ching Rhapsodomancy Stichomancy
Bread	Aleuromancy Crithomancy
Burning	Botanomancy Capnomancy Causinomancy Daphnomancy Pyromancy
Cakes	Alphitomancy
Candles	Lychnomancy
Cards	Cartomancy Tarot
Cats	Ailuromancy
Cheese	Tyromancy

What does the method involve?	See:
Chickens	Alectryomancy
Crystal ball	Crystallomancy
The dead	Necromancy
Donkey	Cephalomancy
Dreams	Oneiromancy
Earth	Geomancy
Entrails	Haruspicy Hepatoscopy Ichthyomancy
Face	Metoposcopy Physiognomy
Fire	Botanomancy Capnomancy Causinomancy Daphnomancy Halomancy Pyromancy Pyroscopy Sideromancy

What does the method involve?	See:
Fish	Ichthyomancy
Flames	Lampadomancy Lychnomancy Pyromancy Sideromancy
Flower	Phyllorhodomancy
Food	Aleuromancy Alphitomancy Crithomancy Cromniomancy Tyromancy

What does the method involve?	See:
Forehead	Metoposcopy
Goat	Cephalomancy
Hands	Chirognomy Chirology Chiromancy Palmistry
Handwriting	Graphology
Head	Phrenology
Hearing	Clairaudience
Horses	Hippomancy
Insects	Entomomancy
Intestines	Haruspicy Ichthyomancy
Key	Cleidomancy
Lamp	Lampadomancy
Leaves	Botanomancy Daphnomancy

What does the method involve?	See:
Lightning	Ceraunoscopy
Liver	Hepatoscopy
Lots	Sortilege
Metal	Molybdomancy
Meteors	Meteormancy
Mice	Myomancy
Mirror	Catoptromancy
Moles	Moleoscopy
Numbers	Arithomancy Numerology Numeromancy

1° 2 3²

What does the method involve?	See:
Oil lamp	Lampadomancy
Onions	Cromniomancy
Paranormal knowledge	Precognition
Pebbles	Pessomancy Psephomancy
Pendulum	Cleidomancy Coscinomancy Radiesthesia
Petals	Phyllorhodomancy
Planets	Astrology
Playing cards	Cartomancy
Poetry	Rhapsodomancy
Pool	Pegomancy
Precious stones	Lithomancy
Reading	Bibliomancy Rhapsodomancy Stichomancy

What does the method involve?	See:
Reflective surface	Catoptromancy Hydromancy Pegomancy Scrying
Ring	Dactylomancy
Rose	Phyllorhodomancy
Salt	Halomancy
Sand	Geomancy
Sheep	Astragalomancy
Shooting stars	Meteormancy
Sieve	Coscinomancy
Skull	Cephalomancy
The sky	Aeromancy Ceraunoscopy Chaomancy Meteormancy
Smoke	Capnomancy Sideromancy

What does the method involve?	See:
Snakes	Ophiomancy
Soil	Geomancy
Space	Astrology
Spiders	Arachnomancy
Spring water	Pegomancy
Stars	Astrology Meteormancy
Stones	Lithomancy Pessomancy Psephomancy
Straws	Sideromancy
Thunder	Ceraunoscopy
Tea leaves	Tasseography
Torch	Lampadomancy
Trance	Metagnomy
Twigs	Dowsing

What does the method involve?	See:
Water	Hydromancy
	Pegomancy
Wax	Ceromancy
The weather	Aeromancy
	Austromancy
	Ceraunoscopy
Wind	Austromancy
	Aeromancy
Wine	Oenomancy
Words	Bibliomancy
	Rhapsodomancy
	Stichomancy
Writing	Graphology

for Operation
thing in the
in a Bank
If I want

INDEX